Introverts

The Ultimate Guide for Introverts Who Don't Want to Change their Quiet Nature but Still Make Friends, Be Sociable, and Develop Powerful Leadership Skills

Contents

Introduction

Do you feel nervous when you are in a crowd? Do you feel scared when you have to talk to strangers? Do your palms start to get sweaty when you are forced to initiate a conversation? If the answer to any of these questions is affirmative, then don't worry. You are not the only one in this world with these feelings about social interaction.

The world can be divided into two kinds of people: outgoing people who love talking and partying, and those who like to be alone and enjoy silence. The first category of people are extroverts, while the second category of people are introverts. If you have chosen to read this book, you are most likely an introvert.

Introverts can often seem quite confusing, while being an introvert can be a daunting experience. Being an introvert in a world ruled by extroverts can feel strange and awkward. It does not matter whether you are young or old, living as an introvert in an extroverted world is difficult.

Introverts must face new problems every day just because the world is too extrovert oriented. This leads to the development of various professional as well as personal problems. For instance, introverts try to avoid professional meetings just because they happen in large, crowded meeting halls. Introverts avoid meeting new people because they do not like clubs or bars, parties, crowded restaurants, etc.

There are many problems that introverts face in their lives, but these problems are not impossible to solve. In fact, they are quite easy to solve if you know how to do it. You just need to apply yourself, and this book will help you do that.

This book contains a detailed analysis of the psyche of introverts and the problems that they face in their day-to-day lives. It contains information regarding introverts and their professional, social, and personal lives. Along with this, the book contains excellent tips that can help you to accept your introversion and become a healthy, sociable individual.

To appeal to everyone, this book has been written in a simple, lucid, and easy to understand manner. This way, even a beginner can understand the mind and life of an introvert. Being an introvert can be hard, but this book will help make your life easier.

Chapter One: Are You an Introvert?

Introversion is a personality type that is often misjudged and misunderstood. This is due to the quiet attitude of introverts. Their silence is often confused for being arrogant or rude. Many people believe that introverts do not like people. This is obviously a false stereotype.

Introverts do not mind people. It is just that they need to take breaks from society to recharge their social energy. Introverts often find it difficult to connect with others and to engage in small talk. They prefer indulging in meaningful conversations instead.

Many people believe that it is only the introverted who feel like living in solitude, but this is a myth. Many extroverts prefer their own company from time to time. Nowadays, people may even be confused about their personality type, i.e., whether they are an introvert or an extrovert. In this section, let us have a look at some signs that can help you assess whether a person is an introvert or not.

Signs of Being Introverted

- Small Talk

Most introverts hate small talk. They tend to avoid circumstances where they might need to indulge in small talk. They do not like discussing random, trivial things such as the weather, trends, etc. Instead, they would rather have a meaningful talk with someone.

- **Overthinking**

A lot of introverts commit the sin of overthinking. This means that a lot of introverts generally overanalyze situations that actually need little analysis.

- **You Like Solitude**

As we mentioned, introverts love solitude. They like spending time with themselves and enjoy activities such as reading, watching movies, writing, listening to music, etc. They would rather spend the weekend alone instead of going to random, noisy parties. Introverts not only like their solitude, but they need it. This is because introverts generally need to recharge their social energy after meeting people.

- **Leadership Qualities**

This might come as a shock to some, but generally, introverts are good leaders. They can not only think deeply but also connect with others on a deeper level. Due to their excellent listening skills, introverts tend to take in everyone's ideas. They like to listen to everyone's plans and point of view instead of being despotic.

- **Networking Issues**

If introverts attend a networking event such as a party or a date, they find it awkward to be there. In parties where you do not know anyone, you may start feeling pressured, stressed, or isolated. Because they do not care for small talk, introverts prefer smaller groups rather than large crowds.

- **Imagination**

Introverts generally possess vivid imaginations. They are creative and like to be ahead of others. The problem that introverts face is expressing their ideas out loud.

- **Phone Talk**

As said above, introverts are not comfortable talking to people on a phone. They would rather text.

- **Center of Attention**

Introverts do not like being the center of attention. They prefer staying on the sidelines, especially in areas where there are a lot of people.

- **You Need Alone Time to Recharge**

Introverts recharge themselves when they are in solitude. They find social events and gatherings exhausting. To recharge themselves, they often escape to silent and serene surroundings.

- **You Are a Good Listener**

Introverts are generally good listeners, because they do not like to impose their ideas and thoughts on other people.

- **Tight-Knit Group**

Introverts generally do not have a lot of friends, but instead perhaps a handful. They tend to be extremely close to these people.

- **Good Observer**

Introverts are generally good observers, and they pay attention to minute details.

- **Anxiety**

Many introverts face anxiety issues. They tend to overanalyze things.

- **Empathetic**

Introverts can not only understand but also relate to the pains of other people. They can understand other people's emotions and can even channel them.

- **Teamwork**

Introverts prefer working alone, but this does not mean that they don't know how to work in teams or groups. They can be excellent leaders if given the opportunity.

- **Creative**

Introverts are generally creative because they have a potent imagination, good observation skills, and emotional sensitivity. They like to look at the world from a different, skillful perspective.

- **Old Soul**

Introverts hate small talk and tend to have more philosophical and deep conversations; therefore, many people call them "old souls."

- **Outgoing Sucks**

Introverts often feel intimidated by outgoing people. They find it difficult to approach and talk to them.

- **Thoughts to Words**

Introverts have a lot of things to say, but they do not know how to say them. They fear misjudgment and being misunderstood. They find it difficult to convey their ideas and thoughts.

- **Sleeping Issues**

Introvert brains are generally overactive. Therefore, introverts do not fall asleep quickly.

- **Crowds are Strange**

Introverts find it difficult to be in a crowd; they tend to feel like they are out of place.

- **People Assume You are Shy**

Introversion does not equal shyness. It is true that introverts do not like socializing a lot, but they are not scared of other people. Shy people find it daunting to socialize with others. And shy extroverts are generally not comfortable being alone most of the time.

- **Initiating Conversations**

Introverts do not like initiating conversations. They find it difficult to start a conversation because they hate small talk. But this does not mean that they do not like talking to people. If someone approaches them, they can generally hold great conversations.

- **Argumentative**

Introverts avoid confrontations and arguments. They do not like snapping at people. They would rather wait and check out the situation before arguing with someone. They like keeping things mellow and quiet.

- Zoning Out

Introverts have highly developed brains, and they are creative. Their imagination is quite active. They generally tend to zone out from time to time whenever crowds or loud noises surround them.

Types of Introversion

The media is full of articles, lists, and stories about the difference between introverts and extroverts. While a lot of information is available about introverts, not many people know that there are four types of introverts. There are a lot of differences between personalities, but according to prevalent theory, there exist four types of introversion: social introversion, anxious introversion, thinking introversion, and restrained introversion. Let us have a look at each.

- **Social Introversion**

Social introversion is the most stereotyped and clichéd of all the introversion types. The social introvert prefers to live alone and does not like to interact with other people. He or she prefers solitude and avoids socializing. His or her group of friends (and close family members) is very small and extremely tight knit.

Social introverts generally find their energy in solitude. They would rather be alone than with a group. Groups drain them mentally, emotionally, and even physically.

Social introversion is often confused with shyness; many people believe that social introverts are shy. But just being a social introvert does not make you shy. Social introverts can be quite outgoing, but they prefer solitude to company. Shy people may be quite outgoing, but they are disinclined to join or socialize with groups.

- **Thinking Introversion**

This type of introvert likes to think about going out and talking to others. For him or her, the world would be perfect if it were as they imagine it could be. These introverts like thinking and analyzing ideas. They like to indulge in nostalgia; they prefer getting lost in their memories and thoughts (but not in a neurotic way).

- **Anxious Introversion**

The third type of introversion is anxious introversion. As the name suggests, the people who have this kind of introversion are generally worried and anxious about situations. They like solitude and enjoy being alone. They tend to feel anxious and awkward when they are in a large crowd, often feeling overly self-conscious.

This kind of introversion is generally related to previous social problems encountered in the course of conversations and interactions. Because of those past experiences anxious introverts tend to find it difficult to relate well to other people. But this does not mean that these past experiences cannot be alleviated; the affected introvert's perspectives can be changed to allow them to feel more comfortable in social situations.

Two methods that can help introverts to alleviate the negative impact of these situations are counseling and therapy. With the help of counseling and therapy, you can rebuild your social confidence.

- **Restrained Introversion**

This is an uncommon form of introversion, not seen as often as other forms of introversion. These introverts find it difficult to relate to other people and to "warm up" to others. They like the company of other people, but only after they get used to the people and the situation. These people are generally known as "reserved". They prefer to think before they speak, and to observe other people before they present their ideas.

While these are the four basic types of introversions there are many more. It is impossible to distinguish all forms of introversion, as they are highly intricate and overlapping. This model can help you understand the basic types of introversion and understand yourself better. But do not use these types to pigeonhole yourself. Generally, people tend to have a mixture of all the above four types. Remember, people are complex, and pigeonholing them into one type will always fetch incorrect results.

Famous Introverts

A lot of people believe that to be successful, you need to have an outgoing personality, i.e., you need to be an extrovert. But this is a myth. In fact, a lot of famous people achieved their success because they were (are) introverted. In this section, let us have a look at some of the most successful and well-known introverts.

- **Albert Einstein**

Albert Einstein is perhaps the most famous scientist and physicist in the world. He was also one of the most renowned introverts. Einstein firmly believed that his knowledge, success, and creativity were all a result of his introversion and habit of introspection. He found new ideas and discovered things when he sat down in solitude.

Like Einstein, you can sit in solitude and enjoy the peace. It will help you think creatively about the tasks that you want to do.

- **Bill Gates**

Bill Gates is one of the richest and most successful people in the world. He is also an introvert. He believes that the tranquility and serenity found in solitude can help a person become successful because solitude allows people to think over their ideas patiently, looking at them from all points of view, and combining the ideas thus sorted out with the energy of extroverts can make a company achieve great success.

Another factor that is worth noticing about Gates is that while he is an introvert, he is not shy. This shows that no one is a true introvert (or true extrovert.)

- **Eleanor Roosevelt**

Eleanor Roosevelt was an iconic public figure who will always be remembered for her press conferences, public lectures, and charismatic personality. So, it may come as a surprise to many people that Roosevelt was an introvert. She was of the firm opinion that it is crucial to be friends with yourself, and that if you cannot be your own friend then you cannot be friends with others. To become friends with yourself, you need to enjoy and relax in solitude.

Solitude allows you to be sensitive about other people and their problems. It allows you to relate to people on a different level. Therefore, introversion can help you connect with others through solitude.

• **Meryl Streep**

Actors are often thought to extroverts because they tend to be outgoing, expressive, and have a lot of confidence. But a surprising number of actors are introverts. One of the brightest examples is Meryl Streep. Meryl Streep is a confident and talented actress, but she likes to enjoy her solitude from time to time. She understands her introverted characteristics and uses them to her advantage.

These examples show that introverts are not superior to extroverts, or vice versa. Both types have their strengths and weaknesses, and it depends on how you use them.

So, introverts are unique in their own way, and you do not need to be hard on yourself for being one. You cannot change yourself and become an extrovert. If you believe your introversion is creating problems in your life, you can change the traits slightly, or like Streep, use your introverted characteristics to your advantage.

You need to remember that no one is thoroughly extroverted or introverted. You need to learn how to adapt to the situations or accept them. Use your creativity and passion to lead the world and live your life to the fullest.

Chapter Two: Introvert Myths

As mentioned, there are many myths associated with introverts. A lot of these mythical stereotypes are harmless, but some of them can hurt your integrity and image. In this section, let us have a look at some myths associated with introversion.

"Introverts are Shy"

Many people believe that introverts are shy and that they do not like interacting with others. This is false. Introverts like interacting with people, but they find it draining, and therefore they don't do it often. Shyness is not an introvert-specific trait. Extroverts can be shy as well.

"Introverts Don't Like People"

Introverts like people as much as extroverts do. But instead of approaching everyone and talking to everyone all the time, introverts tend to be reserved and approach people with caution. Introverts prefer intimate meetings to social occasions. They have few friends, but these friends are extremely close.

"Introverts Lack Social Skills"

Introverts are not socially awkward. They tend to have good social skills. Many times, people view some introverts as extroverts because they are adept at social skills.

"Introverts Lack Thoughts and Ideas"

Having ideas and expressing them are two different things. Introverts find it difficult to express their ideas, but this does not mean that they don't get excellent ones. In fact, many well-known geniuses of the world were introverts. The minds of introverts are like locked books. You need to possess the proper keys to open them, but once open, these books are full of hidden treasures and immaculate knowledge. Introverts tend to think a lot before expressing their views and ideas.

"Introverts Love Solitude"

Introverts indeed love solitude, but they do not always want to be solitary and lonely. Introverts crave intimacy just as much as extroverts. They do not like being lonely; there is a difference between being alone and loneliness.

"Introverts Are Boring"

Introverts are not boring, but they tend to get tired while socializing. Introverts know how to enjoy parties, but they do not like them too much. Introverts can dance, sing, travel, and have fun, too.

"Introverts Are Depressed"

Introverts are not depressed. Introverts like being alone, but this desire is not a sign of depression. The desire to be alone rises out of their desire to restore their energy via quiet time. It is their time to refuel.

"Introverts Are a Minority"

While it is true that there are more extroverted people in this world than introverts, introverts form around 30-40% of the total population.

"Introverts Like Listening, not Speaking"

It is true that introverts are generally great listeners, but this does not mean that they do not like to speak. Introverts enjoy speaking, but they need to be invited to do so. If they are drained, then they prefer listening over speaking.

"Introverts Can't Stand Being Interrupted"

Like every other person, introverts find it exceptionally rude and frustrating when someone constantly interrupts them. When this happens and introverts pause, it does not mean that they have nothing to say; they are just collecting their thoughts.

"Introverts Don't Like Conversations"

Introverts do not like small talk. They do not like to indulge in social pleasantries because they tire of them quickly. Introverts do not like talking on the phone. Unfortunately, disinterest in these activities is often considered to be rude by extroverts. This is because extroverts primarily designed the rules and etiquettes of socializing. While introverts try to be as polite as possible, sometimes it becomes too difficult.

"Introverts Like Loneliness"

The fact that introverts need "me" time is well known. Still, many people feel offended when introverts excuse themselves to be alone. Extroverts often believe that introverts are rude and that they do not like the extrovert, which is why they try to excuse themselves. Instead of taking things personally, extroverts should try to understand the mindset and needs of introverts.

"Introversion Can Be Cured"

This is an extremely offensive myth because it perpetuates the false notion that there is something wrong with introversion, and that it is a disease. Introverts cannot be cured because they are not suffering from any disease. Introverts are perfectly natural.

"Introverts are Judgmental"

Introverts like being silent, causing some people to think that they are judgmental. Introverts tend to think and reflect upon subjects before speaking. Some of them even daydream while being silent. Silence should not be confused with being judgmental.

"Introverts Lack Emotions"

Introverts are not unemotional. They feel all the emotions that extroverts feel, but they express them in a milder form. The feelings, emotions, and expressions of introverts are reserved and inhibited compared to those of extroverts. They do not like to wear their hearts on their sleeves. Introverts share their feelings only with their true friends and people whom they trust.

Chapter Three: Understanding Introverted Personalities

Introversion can be quite confusing, even for introverts themselves. In this chapter, let us have a closer look at introversion and various aspects of introversion.

MBTI

The MBTI or the Myers-Briggs Type Indicator test is a personality test based on the theories of Carl Jung, that divides people into 16 categories. According to this theory, all individuals act in particular ways which can help researchers to divide them into specific categories. People who fall into certain categories display the characteristics of these categories.

The 16 categories are equally divided into introverted categories and extroverted categories. In this section, let us have a look at the introverted personality types.

Personality Types

As explained in the previous chapter, introverted individuals like to indulge in solitude. They prefer thinking things over before they take any action. Many times, introverts are too focused on the idea and the thought processes instead of action. Therefore, many introverts prefer the "idea" of something over the "real thing" itself.

Let us now have a look at the eight MBTI introverted personalities.

- **ISTJ**

Introverted / Sensing / Thinking / Judging

ISTJs are serious, strong, peaceful, and quiet. They prefer the serene beauty of life. If you are an ISTJ individual, you are most likely dependable, responsible, and thorough. Individuals who are ISTJs are highly practical and logical. They are focused and work hard to reach their goals. Sometimes they can be quite the traditionalists. They prefer order over chaos and keep their surroundings as organized as possible.

- **ISFJ**

Introverted / Sensing / Feeling / Judging

These individuals are kind, quiet, and conscientious. They are well-known for being responsible. They like to commit to things and follow through on them. They often put the needs of other people above their own. They are practical and like stability. They are attuned to the feelings of other people, and like helping others.

- **INFJ**

Introverted / Intuitive / Feeling / Judging

INFJs are sensitive, forceful, and original but in a quiet and reserved way. They like to find the meaning of connections between ideas, people, and possessions. They are highly curious. They work hard to understand the motives of other people. They are firm about their decisions and values. They possess clarity of ideas and thoughts. They know how to achieve the common good. They are organized, which helps them implement their clear ideas properly.

- **INTJ**

Introverted / Intuitive / Thinking / Judging

INTJs are supposed to be analytical, independent, determined, and original. They can turn ideas into action. They can detect patterns in external events. When they are committed to things, they will see them through. INTJ individuals have high standards and like to judge their own performance as critically as they do that of others. They have excellent leadership qualities, but they can also work under existing leaders.

- **ISTP**

Introverted / Sensing / Thinking / Perceiving

These individuals are generally reserved and quiet. They like to observe things to understand their workings. They are skilled in mechanical work. Many of these individuals are interested in extreme sports and excel at them. These individuals are tolerant and flexible. Instead of jumping to conclusions immediately, they think things over and observe them from a distance until the solution becomes apparent. Some people find these individuals detached and excessively practical, but their practicality helps them easily find solutions to complex problems.

- **ISFP**

Introverted / Sensing / Feeling / Perceiving

ISFP means one who is kind, quiet, sensitive, and serious. They do not like conflict and rarely engage in things that can lead to disagreements. They are faithful and loyal. They are open-minded and extremely flexible. They are generally creative and original. They like to do work by taking their own time. They appreciate the present and enjoy experiencing it.

- **INFP**

Introverted / Intuitive / Feeling / Perceiving

INFPs are extremely sensitive about their values, and they stay loyal to people whom they admire. They are quiet, reflective, and are often thought to be idealistic. They generally have a highly developed personal-value system, and rarely go against it. They are adaptable, loyal, and laid back, but their laid-back nature disappears as soon as one of their values gets threatened.

- **INTP**

Introverted / Intuitive / Thinking / Perceiving

INTPs are known to be creative, original, and logical. They like theories and ideas and get excited about them. They prefer knowledge, logic, and competence over other aspects. They are reserved and like to be quiet, which is why they often appear to be mysterious. They are lone wolves and do not like following or leading others.

It is clear from all this that there are different types of introverts present in this world. Many people tend to identify with multiple MBTI types. All these types have their own strengths and weaknesses, and none of them is stronger (or weaker) than the others.

Chapter Four: What Does It Feel Like to Be an Introvert?

If you are reading this book, you are either an introvert or an extrovert who is trying to understand the intricacies of introversion. Either way, it is necessary to understand how introverts generally feel. Even introverts sometimes find it difficult to understand their feelings. Dealing with the hardships of life as an introvert can be quite daunting.

Not everyone understands what it feels like to be an introverted person. The world is indeed changing rapidly, and now people have become more accepting, but introverts still form a minority. According to some researchers, only 30% of the total population is introverted. A lot of misconceptions are present about introverts, including a lot of stereotypes and myths. These stereotypes are often so farfetched that they miss the mark totally.

For instance, many people have the misconception that introverts are lonely and shy. They feel that introverts are generally afraid of other people. This, of course, is false. Being an introvert is just like being an extrovert; the experiences are similar but are processed differently.

Being an introvert is no different in this regard than being an extrovert or an ambivert. Many introverts share the same hobbies and activities that extroverts or ambiverts enjoy. These include parties and talking to friends. But there exist some differences in the level of emotions between the two. One of the biggest differences between introverts and extroverts is how they regard solitude.

All individuals need "social energy" to interact with others. Extroverts are like powerhouses of social energy because they receive social energy by being sociable. But introverts cannot do this. Their energy is only recharged when they are alone and solitary. This is why being introverted can often be exhausting.

Introverts like Being Alone

Introverts love being alone. For introverts, solitude does not equal emptiness, boredom, or loneliness. They feel extremely comfortable when alone. They like thinking on their own and pondering things. They enjoy solo activities such as origami, art, drawing, reading, etc. Introverts do not consider solitude "filler time"; for an introvert, solitude is the best time of the day.

If you are an introvert, finding "me time" in today's world can be quite difficult. Finding a quiet and solitary time without interruptions has become difficult. If introverts do not get their "me" time, they may become snappy and frustrated. They need their time to contemplate, like monks, else they find the world too much to handle.

While introverts enjoy their solitude and like spending time with themselves, this does not mean that they do not enjoy the company of other people. Many introverts recharge their social energy by being solitary and then use this energy to interact with each other. Introverts are, after all, human beings, and human beings are social animals. They cannot live without the company of others. They want to interact with others after their "me" time. But the duration of this "me" time differs from individual to individual.

Introverts and Socializing

Extroverts find "alone time" scary and boring. Some extroverts get extremely restless when they are alone for too long. Extroverts feel happy when they are with people; they try to be in the company of other people as much as possible.

For introverts, socializing means a totally different thing. They either do not enjoy it as much as extroverts, or they enjoy it but find it absolutely exhausting.

Certain activities, places, and situations are more tiring than others for introverts. For instance, introverts find large crowds more tiring than smaller ones; they find noisy places more tiring than quiet ones. They find talking to strangers more difficult than talking to people they know.

All social activities wear out introverts. They may enjoy it thoroughly, but they will get quite tired compared to extroverts at the same affair. But this does not mean that there is anything wrong with them. It is just the way they are wired. If you are an introvert, then enjoy your introversion and solitude.

The Effects of Dopamine

Being an introvert is genetic. There is a significant difference between the brains of introverts and extroverts; their brains handle dopamine in different ways. Dopamine is the "reward chemical" of the brain; it is a neurotransmitter that brings in the feeling of ecstasy.

How Dopamine Affects Extroverts

The brains of extroverts are less sensitive to dopamine. This means that they need a lot of outside stimulation to feel happy and energized. Therefore, they tend to enjoy talking, chatting, laughing, smiling, dancing, and spending time with people. They like to keep themselves active and busy.

The brains of introverts are far more sensitive to dopamine as compared to extroverts. They feel satisfied and rewarded quickly. They do not need a lot of stimuli. Therefore, introverts enjoy sitting in solitude and thinking things over, and enjoy spending quiet time with their books. An excessively loud environment like a large crowd will overstimulate the brains of introverts, causing them to tire quickly.

Loud and noisy environments are draining experiences for introverts as well as extroverts. But introverts find it much more draining than extroverts. Extroverts continue to enjoy loud environments because it gives them dopamine. Therefore, they continue to dance, chat, or talk to people.

Chapter Five: Introverts and Quiet Time

Why Do Introverts Love Being Alone?

If you are an introvert, you probably love being alone at times. You probably prefer sitting alone, reading, and thinking to partying all day. You would rather indulge in a thought-provoking conversation than shallow small talk. You prefer spending time alone. A popular meme targeting introverts say that there is nothing better in the world (for introverts) than when their friends cancel plans.

Introverts like and, in fact, *need* alone time because if they don't get it, they become mentally drained. Introverts regain their energy through solitude. If they do not get some solitary time, they tend to get drained mentally and emotionally. They become frustrated, and every little problem and annoyance becomes gigantic for them. They stop functioning properly, their thinking suffers, and even a little annoyance can make them immensely angry or sad. If the situation continues, then they may become physically exhausted or may even fall sick.

All the above things are common all over the world. But these things happen not because introverts are inherently cranky and evil. There are a lot of scientific reasons behind how people act and behave. Dopamine plays an integral role in deciding how we behave in day-to-day life.

Introverts, Extroverts, and Rewards

We do things so that the brain can get enough or, better still, ample amounts of dopamine. As we discussed earlier, extroverts need a lot of dopamine to feel satisfaction and happiness, while the brains of introverts become satiated with little servings. Therefore, many times, the rewards that can motivate and excite extroverts can also tire them.

- **Introverts Don't Need as Much Stimulation**

All this can be boiled down to the simple fact that introverts do not require a lot of stimulation to feel rewarded. The level of stimulation that extroverts enjoy is often too much for introverts. For instance, extroverts love parties because they involve a lot of stimulation, like a lot of people talking together, the chaos, the loud music, lights, crowd, alcohol, etc. For extroverts, this is heaven, but for introverts it's not so heavenly for long. This is because the brains of introverts will get overstimulated, and they will find it difficult to focus anywhere. If you are an introvert caught in a party like this, it is better to escape, go back home, and enjoy a simple dinner while watching TV. It will help you reduce the overstimulation and will make you feel calm and happy once again.

- **The Dopamine Difference**

In the last chapter, we saw how introverts do not care about rewards as much as extroverts do. This is because their tolerance of a neurotransmitter called dopamine. Dopamine is present in our brains, and it is often known as the "reward chemical" or "feel-good" chemical. This is because dopamine is responsible for the reward and pleasure centers of the brain.

Many people believe that socializing is only tiring for introverts, but this is not true. Extroverts feel tired after a lot of socializing as well. Dopamine can help you reduce this stress. But what makes introverts and extroverts different is that dopamine helps extroverts a lot while socializing because it gives them energy boosts from time to time. Extroverts are born with an active dopamine system. Introverts are not blessed with a strong dopamine system, and they feel tired mentally as well as physically after socializing.

Extroverts and People

Extroverts also prefer being with people more than introverts because extroverts place a lot of significance on people. According to a recent study, it was found that extroverts feel highly stimulated when they see and meet new people. Introverts, on the other hand, pay more attention to inanimate objects.

Chapter Six: The Comfort Zone Myth

Everyone believes that if a person wants to succeed, he or she needs to get out of his or her comfort zone. But most of the time, people only say this to introverts. And when they say this, they mean "Become more like extroverts if you want to succeed." This is why that, while it sounds meaningful and important, "comfort zone" is such a loaded and oftentimes problematic term.

Due to the prevalence of this statement, a lot of introverts try to "break out of their shell." They try hard to get out of their "comfort zone." Not only is this a difficult (and perhaps impossible) task, but it is also a harrowing and painful experience. Almost no introvert succeeds in doing this because an introvert can't become an extrovert, nor vice versa. The only thing an introvert can do is become a fake extrovert. But it is an unsustainable decision that takes its toll.

If you, being an introvert, try to get out of your "comfort zone" you will start copying the extroverts around you. Each person and personality type are born with certain assets. For instance, introverts are born with good listening and observation skills. They think and analyze things before making decisions. But when you try to come out of your "comfort zone," you start forgoing these skills and replacing them with pseudo-extrovert characteristics. But adopting the strength of another personality type is not simple. You cannot take over these skills and hope for the best. You may even lose your own assets while trying to gain these new ones. Ultimately, it is far better to play to your strengths instead of changing things around all the time.

What is a Comfort Zone?

As said above, the comfort zone is a loaded term with a lot of meanings and definitions. But in simple words, the comfort zone includes situations, people, skillsets, and places in which a person feels comfortable, competent, and safe. It includes all the circumstances that you find enjoyable and pleasing. The edge of the comfort zone is a confusing place. It is as if you have one foot in the "uncomfortable zone" and one foot in the "comfort zone." People generally find this zone more complex and challenging than their comfort zone. While you can handle situations in this zone without too much anxiety and other such problems, it is still much more difficult than the comfort zone. Anything beyond this zone is considered to be "out of your comfort zone."

But this is a shallow understanding of the comfort zone concept, because situations that need a lot of talking, robust actions, and interactions are the extroverts' comfort zone. As explained in the previous chapter, the brains of extroverts and introverts handle dopamine differently. Extroverts feel comfortable and happy when exciting things surround them. They are wired like that. They like to jump into the action right away. They don't get tired from meeting new people, and they enjoy the hustle and bustle of the world. This is why extroverts feel comfortable while visiting large meetings, parties, and conventions. As a lot of people in this world are extroverts, most of the social conventions are designed to accommodate them. Therefore, introverts are forced to get out of their comfort zone and enter the comfort zones of extroverts. This is a discriminating situation because introverts will never succeed in tackling these environments because introverts will always be the outsiders in the comfort zones of extroverts.

Extroverts exhibit being comfortable on the outside, but introverts feel comfortable on the inside. The comfort zone of introverts is inside their mind. They feel comfortable in situations that require a lot of planning, thinking, and precision. This is because their nervous system is wired that way. They prefer to rest and understand things properly before making decisions. If introverts do not get their alone time to reflect and introspect, they feel drained. They find large and noisy crowds overwhelming. Their thinking clouds in such situations. This is why introverts tend to avoid the spotlight.

Unlike extroverts, introverts find solace and comfort in small gatherings, quiet places, and in solitude. They do not feel comfortable with strangers and would rather talk to the people they know. They do not need a lot of outside stimuli. Instead, they prefer the calmness and soothing sounds of nature.

But, as we have seen, the extroverts run the world (allegedly), and they decide the rules, which is why introverts are often forced to come out of their comfort zones and enter the zones of extroverts. Many researchers believe that, like extroverts, if introverts can work while being in their own comfort zone, it can work wonders toward making the endeavors more successful.

Complacent Zone

When people tell introverts (and extroverts, too) to come out of their comfort zone, they mean the complacency zone. The complacency zone is different from the comfort zone, and it would be nice if everyone started using the term "complacency zone" instead of "comfort zone". The term comfort zone now has many negative connotations, and it's better to avoid the term altogether.

Everyone needs to get out of their complacency zone if they want to succeed. The complacency zone is the zone in which we tend to seek shelter from the problems of the world. This zone allows us to maintain a false status quo which helps us feel safe. But safety hinders your progress. You cannot grow if you do not take risks and remain hiding in a safe house most of the time. The complacency zone only provides you with a false sense of security and safety. It is false because it only leads to failure and stagnation. You will get stuck in a place or position if you don't take risks.

When a person is in the complacency zone, he or she will try to invoke a variety of rationales to justify his or her presence in the zone. If you ever want to succeed, you need to start listening to your inner voice. If it's making excuses for you constantly occupying your complacency zone, it may be time for some adjustments.

Working from the Comfort Zone

Almost all extroverts work from their comfort zone, while introverts are often forced out of theirs. Pulling a crab out of its shell kills it; pulling an introvert out of his or her comfort zone hinders his or her abilities significantly. Once introverts understand that they can perform their best while being in their comfort zone, they will never want to come out of it. This is excellent because their comfort zone will allow them to be free, excited, creative, and enthusiastic.

But remember, do not confuse your comfort zone with your complacency zone. You need to get out of your complacency zone but stay in your comfort zone. This will help you to move forward in your personal and professional life.

Chapter Seven: Introverts and Mental Health

Mental Issues Faced by Introverts and Extroverts

Mental health is a complex topic. Whether introvert or extrovert, mental health issues can plague anyone. Both personality types need to pay close attention to their mental health.

As said in the previous chapter, introverts are often considered shy because they like solitude and spending time with themselves. But excessive isolation can lead to the development of a lot of problems. Excessive isolation is a sign of depression and many other mental health issues.

Extroverts generally like to spend a lot of time surrounded by people. But an overdose of this can turn an individual into an excessively clingy person. Both personality types face their own problems.

Introverts especially should stay cautious. They can often become too isolated. There is a huge difference between solitude and loneliness. If you constantly isolate yourself from other people, it can lead to the development of various mental diseases and disorders such as social anxiety and depression. In fact, excessive isolation is a potent symptom of depression. If you feel that you like isolation too much, then you should check whether your need for isolation is a result of a lack of energy or has some other serious underlying cause. Other serious mental disorders that can lead to (and arise from) excessive isolation include addictions, personality problems, and eating disorders. An introverted person should always have a strong support system consisting of people whom they can trust. If you are an introvert who likes solitude a lot, talk to your friends and try to form a group that can keep a check on you. If you do not have close friends with whom you can share your emotions and vulnerable thoughts, then it is time to find some.

You also need to establish whether you are really an introvert or not. Sometimes people get introversion confused with social and anxiety-related disorders.

A personal assessment is crucial to avoid problems in this area; if you believe that your discomfort is a result of social anxiety, then it is recommended you contact a therapist or a mental health professional as soon as possible.

While isolation is the major problem related to introversion, many other problems can become serious as well. Introverts are generally more susceptible to depression than extroverts. Neurological studies have proven that the brain activity of introverts is stronger and more intense than the brain activity in extroverts. This is why introverts do not need as many stimuli as extroverts. Having an active brain is a great thing because it allows introverts to be creative, thoughtful, and innovative. But an overactive brain can lead to various other problems. For instance, if you have an overactive brain, you will tend to overthink a lot, leaving you feeling overwhelmed. It is also bad for people who tend to get over-emotional. Overthinking is especially bad if you obsess over negative ideas and thoughts. This problem becomes even more severe when the person is secluded and prefers living in isolation. Seclusion bottles up these emotions of pain and despair, and this bottling up results in the development of feelings such as hopelessness, shame, guilt, helplessness, and worthlessness. These feelings act as a gateway to more severe mental health issues.

Ultimately, there is nothing wrong with being an extrovert or an introvert. Both have their particular characteristics, and both of them have their pros and cons. Both personality types share the same mental health problems. Mental health issues should not be taken as a sign of weakness. Mental disorders are just like any other disorder. You just need to check for the symptoms from time to time. If you believe that you have symptoms of any mental health disorder, it is recommended you contact a health professional as soon as possible.

Why Should Introverts Have a Health Plan?

Introverts love quiet time. Whenever they are in solitude, introverts tend to be more productive and reliable. They tend to get brilliant ideas when they are left alone. They can accomplish a lot of things if they are allowed to have their time, silence, and space. But solitude can be a curse as well. If introverts live in solitude a lot, their minds can take over and start thinking negatively. This can lead to the development of various psychological issues. Many times, introverts become overwhelmed because they cannot control their psychological problems and negative ideas. Additionally, the typical Introverts' creativity intensifies the problem.

This phenomenon is seen in many introverts all over the world. It can lead to the development of a mental crisis which can be quite difficult to deal with. So, there are certain mental health precautions that every introvert must take. If you, as an introvert, do not have a medical emergency plan, you may end up in a psychiatric ward. In this section, let us have a look at why you should always have a proper mental health plan in place.

- **Introverts and Expanded Psychiatric Services**

Introverts need to have an emergency mental health plan because they are more likely than extroverts to face a mental health emergency. In 2010 two researchers, Laurie Helgoe and Nancy Ancowitz, came up with an article suggesting that the American Psychological Association should include introversion as a significant factor in the diagnosis of personality disorders. Introverts spend a lot of time thinking; if the thoughts are positive, it does not matter much, but if their mind is full of negative thoughts, it can overwhelm them. They may become antisocial. In some extreme cases, people have become agoraphobic. These and many other related problems can lead to the development of mental health emergencies. Introverts must study the signs and symptoms of the most common mental disorders. Along with knowing these symptoms, they should also have an action plan that can help in tackling mental health emergencies.

• **Emergency Psych Services (U.S.) and Silence**

The psych services available in the United States of America are not introvert friendly. These services are rarely private or quiet. As introverts require their share of peace and seclusion every day, a noisy and excessively public place can aggravate their symptoms. Instead of helping, these services can often exacerbate problems.

This is why many introverts avoid getting help for their problems; they are worried about the environment in which they will have to live. But various options can help you avoid this environment and still get treatment. For instance, if the problem is not too severe, you can leave the place after spending a night. If you set up these things before the problem arises, you will have everything planned, and you will not be left at the mercy of the staff. Some new psych services consider the needs and requirements of introverts and try to provide a friendly and comfortable atmosphere for them. Try to locate a service like this near you. If you cannot find one, then use the "overnighter" option.

• **Introverts and a Tiny Social Circle**

One of the biggest differences between introverts and extroverts is their social circle. Extroverts tend to have a large social circle. This way, if ever an emergency or crisis arises, they can have a lot of friends who can help them, and their friends will call other people to help.

This is not feasible in the case of introverts. Introverts generally have a small social circle. They do not have a lot of friends. While the quantity of relationships for introverts is low, the quality is exceptionally good. This is because introverts tend to spend a lot of time with the same people, which results in the development of stronger relationships, attachments, and connections. This is why you need to make your friends aware of your problems. You need to choose your contacts carefully so that they can rush to help you. If you are in a mental health emergency situation, you will be confused and will not understand what to do. It is therefore recommended that you let your friends know about your problem beforehand so that if an emergency comes up, they will have control over the situation.

- **Introverts and Ignoring Health Problems**

It is a well-known fact that introverts are private individuals who do not like talking a lot about themselves. They love being left to their own devices, which is why many introverts avoid going to their doctors regularly. This is because doctors tend to ask a lot of questions of the patients. Introverts do not particularly like answering questions about their personal life, especially if there is nothing wrong with them. But that's how doctors work. This is why you need to have a regular mental as well as physical checkup to avoid any surprise diseases and disorders. A regular mental health checkup will help you avoid a sudden anxiety attack or will at least keep you prepared for one.

- **Preventing Attacks**

If you are an introvert, you may feel overwhelmed from time to time. You may also feel that your emotions are holding you back. But this does not mean that you cannot live a healthy and fulfilling life. Introverts often feel lost, especially in cases such as anxiety attacks and panic attacks. While that is not the case with all introverts, everyone needs to have a plan to keep things under control. This will help prevent a full-blown panic or anxiety attack. Remember that knowledge is power.

If you feel that you may fall prey to a mental health problem in the future, you should be vigilant at all times. You need to care for yourself and your mental health. Let us have a look at some tips that can help you keep your mind sound and sharp.

Professional Advice

Everyone visits a dentist or a physician for annual checkups; you should form a habit of visiting a mental health professional to get yourself checked out from time to time. It is true that this is a costly affair, but if money is not an issue for you, then you can find a decent psychiatrist or psychologist who can help you immensely.

If money is an issue, then check whether your insurance covers mental health professionals. This will allow you to get help at a low cost.

If your insurance does not cover mental health, then try seeking other options such as public assistance.

If you ever feel inclined to cause yourself harm, call 911 in the U.S. (999 in the U.K.) as soon as possible. Remember, your life is more important than money.

Know Yourself

Introverts love seclusion, and they spend a lot of time alone. This is why, when something goes wrong with them, people around them rarely notice it. If you tend to spend a lot of time alone, then you need to know yourself properly. This means you should be able to understand yourself and your general behavior patterns. If you ever begin acting differently, you will notice the change quickly.

Emergencies and Non-Emergencies

You need to have a proper plan related to emergencies and non-emergencies. You should know where to go or whom to meet if emergency situations arise. For instance, if you have a mental health emergency, you may find it difficult to think clearly, so know beforehand which friend(s) you should contact as soon as possible. Dealing with a worst-case scenario can be easier if you have the best plan ready.

Making a mental health plan takes a lot of time and effort, but in the end, it is worth it. Instead of wasting a lot of money and time later, it is better to put in some effort now.

Caution

The suggestions given in this chapter are precautionary. Do not consider them medical recommendations. You should always talk to a medical professional before changing your routine drastically. And do not self-medicate.

Chapter Eight: 15 Ways to Increase Happiness as an Introvert

If you feel bad about being an introvert, don't worry; you are not alone. Many introverts wish that they could be more like their extroverted peers. Extroverts do not feel mentally and physically drained after meeting or socializing with people.

But as you now know, introversion is perfectly natural; there is nothing wrong with being an introvert. The only problem that you may face frequently is how to be happy in an extroverted world. But don't worry; this chapter contains brilliant tips that can help you be content and stay happy.

Time is Essential

Introverts need a lot of time to recover after attending networking events and parties; they also need time to recover after doing ordinary things like shopping in a crowded place, enjoying a heated discussion, or having a stressful day at work. After such occasions, introverts need some time to think and recover. This unwinding time is necessary as it allows them to calm down and relax. If introverts do not get their "me" time, they feel tired, unwell, and "brain-dead".

Meaningful Conversation

Introverts do not care for meaningless conversation; they feel uncomfortable when someone tries making small talk with them.

Many introverts learn the art of small talk, but they nonetheless perform it with mild discomfort. Most introverts do not like talking, but if you are one of those who do, try to find partners with whom you can have meaningful conversations. Meaningful conversations will keep you happy and contented.

But don't worry, meaningful conversations do not mean that you need to ask each other soul-searching questions all the time. Sometimes you may feel like talking about random things such as what your partner did over the weekend. This doesn't mean that you care much for small talk; you still need a meaningful conversation from time to time to keep you afloat.

Companionable Silence

While this point may counter the last one, it is true. As an introvert, you need some quiet "me" time now and then. If you are comfortable with a person, you can enjoy sitting next to them while saying nothing. Introverts do not mind if there are a lot of pauses in a conversation; silence is golden for introverts.

Hobbies and Interests

Introverts generally have many hobbies. Many introverts are highly interested in gardening, reading, cooking, painting, writing, mythology, etc. Introverts generally like to delve deep into their hobbies. Hobbies are a great way to recharge energy.

A Quiet Space

Every introvert likes to have a quiet sanctuary in his or her house. They need a quiet, private space to get away from the hustle and bustle of life. If you have such a room in your house, decorate it according to your whims. In this room, you should feel comfortable and happy. There should not be frequent interruptions in this room.

Time to Think

Introverts need time to think. According to Dr. Laney, introverts use their long-term memory more than their working memory. This is the opposite of extroverts. Many introverts find it difficult to express themselves because they need some time to think over things before expressing them. If introverts are not allowed to think over things before speaking, they may find the situation uncomfortable.

Friends Who Understand

Introverts do not mind socializing, but they need it to happen on their terms. Introverts love their friends, but they prefer people who can let them be themselves.

Work

Instead of working just for money, introverts will always prefer a career that they can enjoy. Introverts are rarely content with something that does not satisfy them intellectually. Introverts crave work, and they want their lives to have a purpose. They don't want a job that pays them well but does not satisfy those other needs.

Permission to Remain Silent

Introverts prefer to stay silent rather than talk. You must have felt like this before; sometimes you do not want to interact with someone because you just do not have the energy to do so. But people rarely let introverts be themselves. If you have understanding friends, they will accept that you need to stay silent from time to time.

Independence

Introverts like being independent and unique. They prefer to do things on their own terms. Introverts feel the happiest and most satisfied when they are allowed to work according to their terms. Introverts like to be self-dependent, independent, and self-reliant.

The Simple Life

Introverts like to lead simple lives. They like situations where they can care for others. They need significance in their life; they do not like living a life that has no meaning.

Friends and Loved Ones

Everyone needs people in their life who can understand and accept them despite their foibles and quirks. Introverts do not like being the center of attention, which is why they struggle in large groups. Many times, they disappear in large crowds because they like to hide in a corner. Introverts want nothing more than having a few good friends who understand them and care for them. Introverts know that they can be difficult to "grok" sometimes, but if their friends understand this and still stick with them, they will be the happiest people in the world.

See Your Whole Self

It bears repeating that no one is totally introverted or extroverted. Personality is a broad spectrum, and everyone has some characteristics of introversion as well as extroversion. People who are totally (or even strongly) introverted or extroverted are rare. Most of the people around us fall somewhere towards the middle of this spectrum. This means that people like to socialize sometimes, and sometimes they tend to avoid crowds and prefer to sit alone instead. If a person lies very near the middle of this spectrum, such people are known as *ambiverts.*

All of us are born with the capability to recharge ourselves through social gatherings, interactions, and affiliation; everyone has some tendency to recharge their energy through solitude and serenity. It is thus necessary to be as honest as possible with yourself. If you feel that you just want to sit alone and talk to no one, do it. If you want to go out and have a talk with a friend or go to a party, then do it. Ultimately, you should do whatever makes you feel happy.

Embrace Your Strengths

Each personality type is born with its own unique strengths. Introverted behavior has a lot of positives. For instance, introverts are often better at solving problems and thinking. They tend to be well-behaved and perform tasks well. They are generally academically gifted. They like taking risks, but they usually only take risks that won't backfire.

According to research, introverts have a lot of gray matter in their prefrontal cortex. This area is present in the front area of the brain. It controls things such as abstract thinking, complex emotions, and decision-making. This is why introverts are blessed with good thinking powers.

In many theological, philosophical, and classical schools of thought, true happiness is said to be derived from spending time alone in contemplation. Ancient thinkers, from Buddha to Aristotle, popularized this notion. Introverts are already blessed with an inclination toward this truism, as they tend to naturally find solace in solitude. Instead of hiding your introvert characteristics, accept them and celebrate them.

Act the Part

According to research, when introverts come face to face with extroverts, they tend to monitor their behavior and try to act like extroverts. This is due to the social pressure to appear positive and accepting. But this experience is quite uncomfortable for the introvert, who feels they need to fake things and be on their toes at all times. According to this research, if introverts act like themselves without any pressure to be someone they are not, they can be happier. (This obviously pretty much applies to every personality group.)

These are some of the methods that can help you to be happy and stay happy as an introvert. Try them for yourself and adopt the ones that work for you.

Chapter Nine: Conquering Introvert Fears and Phobias

One of the biggest problems that an introvert must face is having to deal with fear and nervousness. According to research, an introverted brain generally tries to find security and safety, which is why even the smallest dangers can make your brain hyperactive. Introverted brains are more sensitive to strong feelings, as they concentrate more on inner sensations. This is why introverts feel fear deeply.

Many people think fear is bad and that it is a highly negative sensation. But this is not true; it is not inherently negative. Like every feeling, it is a reaction to the stimulation received from the outside world or the inside workings. The problem with fear begins when it starts to become excessive. When you start to obsess with fear, it usually interferes with your crucial tasks. That's why introverts often freeze up while socializing.

According to some researchers, human beings are born with only two fears: darkness and loud noises. All the other phobias and fears that we tend to have are later developments. No one is free of fear; everyone is afraid of something. Many introverts are generally shy and socially anxious; these two are forms of fear. If you have these fears, then this chapter will help you overcome them. Let us have a look at some tips and methods that can be used to tackle fear.

Small Talk

There are very few introverts in this world who like small talk. The majority of introverts feel uncomfortable making small talk. Introverts generally hate idle conversation; they find it pointless, which is why they tend to become nervous and start fidgeting.

Many introverts try to indulge in small talk by planning it extensively in their minds, but when they try to express themselves, their mouths go dry and their minds go blank. Introverts do not mind talking as a concept; in fact, many introverts love talking about things that really matter or the things that they find interesting. Introverts prefer chats that can help them connect with the situation or the person in a deeper way.

If you are an introvert who is often called "quiet" or "reserved," it is not because you are shy but because you do not find small talk to be interesting. You find it unimportant and irrelevant. You would rather use your energy in some other endeavor instead of wasting it on small talk.

Meeting New People

Many times, introverts feel scared and nervous when meeting and interacting with strangers. Meeting new people is a great way to make new contacts, but it can be quite a task for introverts. Introverts find the initial stages of any relationship (not just romantic ones) quite difficult.

Introverts are especially uncomfortable in large groups and crowds, and they find it difficult to talk to someone while they are in a crowd. If you feel nervous about introducing yourself to someone, don't worry; just try to relax. If you prefer meeting and interacting with people one on one, don't worry; you are not the only one. Many introverts prefer private conversations to overcrowded interactions. No wonder many introverts find starting new jobs difficult.

Big Crowds

Introverts tend to avoid big crowds but sometimes it is impossible to do so. If you are afraid of meeting strangers, then it is likely that you will be afraid of large crowds as well. A crowd of strangers can be particularly troublesome for introverts who suffer from anxiety problems. As said above, introverts generally gain social and personal energy from solitude; crowds drain their energy quickly. Introverts prefer talking and interacting in small groups. If you find yourself caught in a crowd, try to encircle yourself with your friends. This will make you feel slightly more comfortable and may prevent a panic attack.

Talking on The Phone

If you do not like talking on the phone and get nervous when answering it, then don't worry; you are not alone. In fact, this problem is so common that there is a proper term for it, called *telephonophobia*. Some introverts dislike phone calls altogether, but some find only strangers' calls problematic. Some introverts do not find receiving calls troublesome, but they become immensely nervous when they are asked to initiate a call. Some introverts tend to avoid calls from unknown numbers.

There is no particular reason why you may find phone calls difficult and nerve-wracking. Some people believe it is because you cannot see the person with whom you are talking, and so you cannot study his or her body language. This dissociation between the voice and the body can be quite unsettling to many. Introverts are well known for their skills of observation, so when they are forced to speak on the phone, that skill cannot be employed; this may make them panic.

Long Social Engagements

People often try to coax introverts to parties and similar social events by promising them that it will be fun. "Fun" is a subjective term that changes meaning from individual to individual. Thus, what is fun for an extrovert may not be fun for an introvert. In fact, it may be the opposite of fun for him or her.

Introverts love having a good time with their friends, but they would rather do it on their own terms. They dislike wasting their time at parties, especially if they are long and time-consuming parties. These parties are boring to an introvert and can be quite stressful. If you dislike these activities, it is better to let your friends know about your views. If your friends truly love you, they will try to understand your problem.

Embarrassment

Your introversion will definitely play an integral role in your fear of humiliation. Introverts generally spend a lot of time listening and observing. They usually tend to avoid other people because they don't want to be seen or heard doing something that people will remember negatively. Introverts are highly intuitive. This intuition makes them think of a lot of scenarios about the future and things that may or may not take place. Many times, this speculation forces introverts to take a step back and avoid the situation altogether. This is also true because many times, introverts tend to think about the worst-case scenario. While intuition is a great thing, it is better to be prepared to avoid any mishaps. If you get embarrassed easily, it is better to avoid situations that can be humiliating. Try not to draw a lot of attention to yourself. But if you want to conquer the fear of humiliation, the best way is to stop caring. This may be quite difficult in the beginning, but with enough time and practice, you will become shameless, which means you will stop caring about what other people think and feel.

Never let other people judge you for being an introverted person. It is a natural thing; that is why you should accept and embrace all your natural, introverted characteristics. You cannot conquer your fears if you cannot face them. When you learn how to conquer and face your fears, you start to grow as a human being. So, try to tackle your fears, even if they seem too nerve-wracking right now. You can tackle all your introversion-related fears, including shyness, small-talk related nervousness, and fear of embarrassment if you spend some time practicing the methods given in this book.

Learn How It Functions

Before countering any strong foe, you need to understand its weaknesses and strengths. You need to have thorough information about it. If fear is interfering in your life, how does it do it? For instance, it can interfere with your professional life, your academic life, and your personal life. You need to understand the physical signs of psychological as well as physical fear. Once you collect all this information, you can start tackling it properly and become more capable of defeating your fear.

Along with the above information, you should also collect raw data from sources such as articles, books, psychology blogs, and mental health professionals.

Be Aware of Your Fear

Once you collect information related to your fear and become familiar with it, you need to start examining how you feel about it. Understand where you feel it in your body. Do you feel it in your throat, chest, or belly? Understand its physicality, so that next time, when you experience it, you will be able to identify it immediately. This way, you will be able to work against it properly. Naming your fear and calling it aloud from time to time will help you tackle it.

Face It

It is crucial to understand and accept your fear. Do not try to deny it or hide it. Introverts often must deal with negative feelings which they try to hide. But hiding these feelings cannot help because hiding does not solve the underlying problem but is only likely to further aggravate the issue. Once you start noticing and not hiding the fear, you can start tackling it by using the various steps given above. It may indeed seem like a difficult task in the beginning, but with patience, dedication, and time you will be able to do it. Don't be too hard on yourself. You need to tackle your fear gradually. If your first attempt does not go as expected, don't worry, just keep pushing. Fear is a sort of habit, and it is difficult to overcome habits. Even the tiniest step will help you progress. With time you will see the new habits taking root. Once these habits settle in, you won't have to make any effort to maintain them in the future.

Remember Why It Matters

Introverts are often surprised when they see extroverts being happy and joyful even in the scariest social scenarios. One of the biggest reasons why extroverts do not appear to be scared is because of how their brains handle social situations. For them, the social situations are pleasurable, and the feeling of pleasure overpowers the feeling of fear.

Introverts are highly concentrated on their feelings, which is why their fear seems to appear bigger than that of extroverts. This is why they tend to avoid social gatherings. But if this is hindering your progress, you need to get over it. Social interactions are crucial while living in society. You need to ask yourself every time before avoiding something whether it is important or not, whether you need to interact with the person or the situation or not, and whether the current conversation will help you in the future or not.

If you do not partake in the current conversation, will it hinder your prospects in the future? Understanding and answering these questions will help you to calm down and think the matter over carefully. It will also help you control and manage your decisions properly. Remember, your conscience is quite selective, so use it carefully. Try to seek a balance between the pros and cons of the situation and then make a solid decision.

Repeat!

Human beings form habits quickly and then stick to the habits for a long time. Our brain forms habits because they help you to manage things more easily. This mechanism is crucial because it allows the brain to save energy for future tasks, as it can use past experiences to reference your response to present challenges. But for this to work properly, you need to concentrate on every situation so that your brain can form patterned responses to past experiences. If your brain forms bad habits, you will suffer in the future. To make your brain strong, you need to put in conscious effort to drive your behavior carefully. You also need to learn how to adjust your behavior so that you can move forward. Remember, perfection is not possible, but this does not mean that you should stop pursuing it.

Fear is a confusing feeling because its main motive is to warn people about impending danger. Our body, when it senses fear, tends to address it with the instinctive flight-or-fight response. Introverts generally choose the first reaction and try to avoid the situation altogether. It is therefore crucial to manage your internalized fear and move forward in the world.

Chapter Ten: Overcoming Social Anxiety and Awkwardness

People often confuse introversion with social anxiety, especially in the case of extroverts who think all introverts are socially awkward. But introversion and social anxiety are distinctly different and mutually exclusive. In this chapter, let us have an in-depth look at social anxiety and introversion.

First, it is necessary to clarify that introversion is not an illness. Introversion is related to how our body uses energy. Social awkwardness and anxiety are related to how you feel in your day-to-day life and how you respond to things you experience. Let's take a look at how to deal with life experiences if you are an introvert who suffers from social anxiety.

Dealing with Social Anxiety as an Introvert

• Meeting New People

Meeting new people can be difficult, especially for people who have social anxiety. They become obsessed with small details and are generally nervous about making a good impression. This nervousness is also reflected in the content of the conversation, where socially anxious people tend to ask more questions than answer them. This is a great tactic in the initial stages because everyone likes to talk about themselves, but it becomes old quickly. People who have social anxiety generally find it difficult to initiate a conversation because they tend to overthink things, which sometimes makes them appear tongue-tied.

- **Talking is Fun**

In some respects, socially awkward people are quite similar to introverts. Like introverts, socially awkward people to like to talk if the topic is right up their alley. If the topic is interesting, they can talk a lot about it. Introverts and socially awkward people both tend to think a lot before talking. They prefer to collect themselves and gather information before presenting their point of view. But socially awkward people prefer to listen to other people talk. They can talk to multiple people for a fairly long time, but once their threshold is crossed, they start to melt down.

- **Crowds**

Introverts and socially awkward people will usually try to avoid meeting people in a crowded area. The waiting and small-talk aspect of having dinner in a crowded place can be quite nerve-wracking for people who suffer from social anxiety. They will forget to enjoy the meal and the company, and their focus will be on escaping the situation as soon as possible. So instead of going for a crowded place, socially awkward people should choose a calm and serene place with little to no crowds.

- **Quietness**

Extroverts are often bemused by introverts and socially awkward people being so quiet most of the time. Socially awkward introverts can be insanely quiet; they can maintain their silence even in the most difficult situation, because they enjoy it. They have hobbies that generally involve solitude, such as writing, reading, listening to music, gardening, etc. Being silent helps introverts and socially anxious people to concentrate and contemplate. It provides them a sense of the world that allows them to enjoy the little pleasures of life properly.

- **Books**

Many introverted, socially awkward people are avid readers. These people enjoy the company of books a lot. They tend to talk about books a lot. They always have book recommendations for people. They also like to reread the books that they loved because it gives them a sense of reconnection.

Many times, these people disconnect from the world to enter the reality of the book they are reading. They would rather spend hours on end with their book instead of going to a noisy and crowded party.

• **Sadness**

Due to their inherent tendency to feel emotions intensely, introverts who are socially awkward are often sad. Any simple piece of news can trigger them and can make them sad for a long time. Anxiety is often a gateway to depression. Sometimes introverts try to get out of their sadness by being solitary, but many times this solitude can aggravate the problem. When introverts suffering from social anxiety get triggered, their emotional system collapses.

Thus, introversion and social anxiety may seem mutually exclusive, but a person can have both simultaneously. Being an introvert or a socially anxious person is not a negative thing. It just means that you need to keep an eye on your health and work carefully. Introversion is not a mental illness, but according to many sources, social anxiety is. If you have both, then it is necessary to be bold and be confident. There is nothing wrong with you. You may indeed find certain situations and aspects of your life quite difficult, but it does not mean that you should sit in a corner moping. Be yourself and be yourself confidently! It does not matter if you are an introvert or that you are anxious. Just be bold.

Differences between Social Anxiety and Introversion

In the previous section, we saw how to deal with social anxiety and introversion together. But what are the major differences between these two? In this section, let us have a look at these differences in detail.

- **Introversion is Born; Social Anxiety is *Made***

Introversion is perfectly natural, and it is a part of your personality. You cannot change it, and you cannot cure it because it is not a disease or a disorder. Introversion comes directly from the womb. Socially awkward people are generally introverted but while these two are mutually exclusive, many times introverts tend to be socially awkward because of the lethal combination of genetics and social experiences.

Many things can make a person socially anxious. One of the major reasons why a person can be socially anxious is learning. People tend to learn new things in different new situations, and sometimes the things that they learn are negative. For instance, if your parents are always worried about something, you may learn to worry, cultivating that habit in your mind. This trait then gets enhanced by actions and experiences such as bullying and other such traumatic interactions. People who have social anxiety often tend to think that they are just not up to the mark.

Another aspect of social anxiety is avoidance of interaction. People who have social anxiety tend to avoid things because they do not want to indulge in small talk. They make excuses and even feign illness. In parties, if these people feel nervous, they stare at their phones constantly to avoid interacting with others. Some may even avoid meeting people at parties by hiding in the bathroom.

- **Fear of Being Revealed**

People who have social anxiety tend to believe that there is something inherently wrong with them. This is because they do not believe in themselves, and they believe that they have a lot of flaws that they have kept hidden; most of the time, these supposed flaws are fake and do not exist, yet they convince themselves that they have these flaws.

These flaws can be of a varied nature; they can be physical as well as mental. For instance, they may believe that they turn red when they talk to people, and their palms start to sweat. Some people may feel that the world will laugh at them if they try to voice their opinions. It does not matter what flaws these people think they have; they are scared of them being revealed.

The introverts who do not have social anxiety do not believe that there is something inherently wrong with them. They are not scared about the "big reveal" because they have nothing in particular to hide.

• **Perfectionism and Social Anxiety**

Perfectionism is the bane of human existence. People who strive for perfection apparently do not realize that perfection does not exist. People who have social anxiety try to achieve perfection in social interactions; they try to be as socially flawless as possible. They have an all-or-nothing attitude, which in itself is quite problematic. Socially anxious people are afraid of criticism. They try to be charming and witty to avoid criticism, but it does not always work. When it does not work, it may mentally paralyze the person.

Introverts who do not suffer from social anxiety do not care about these things. They understand that they are not always under the scrutiny of others. They do not anticipate judgment. They tend to follow the natural flow in the conversation. But even if the conversation does not flow naturally and ends up being awkward, they won't think too much about it because ultimately, they do not care that much about how it went.

• **Introversion is Your Way; Social Anxiety *Gets in Your* Way**

Social anxiety is closely related to fear. In fact, social anxiety is almost always channeled through fear. People who have social anxiety tend to avoid gatherings and large crowds because they fear the noise. But some extroverts who are socially anxious can also feel this way. Extroverts love parties, and if social anxiety does not allow them to visit one, they will feel frustrated and angry. If social anxiety is bringing new problems into your life almost every day, then it is recommended you do something about it.

Like socially anxious people, introverts also try to avoid parties; if they end up at a party, they try to leave it as soon as possible. Unlike socially anxious people, they do not care if they leave too early. They do not criticize themselves for leaving early because they know that they just don't find partying interesting enough. They do not judge themselves or feel strange, either. Their choice is not driven by fear; it is only driven by their judgment and mind.

Thus, social anxiety may seem like a kind of introversion in the beginning, but if you delve deep, you will realize that these two things are quite different. But it is possible to overcome social anxiety. You just need to learn how to do it. In the next chapter, we'll have a look at how you can be socially confident even if you are socially awkward.

Chapter Eleven: How to Be Socially Confident

Being socially confident is not a difficult task. With some practice, time, and dedication, anyone can be socially confident. If you tend to avoid social gatherings or sit in a corner when you attend one, don't worry; you are not the only one. There are many people like you in the world, whether introverted or not. Solving this problem is quite easy. You just need to be confident and bold. Let us have a look at how you can become a self-confident and socially adept person in a few simple steps.

Creating a Confident Outlook

- **Accept Yourself**

If you do not accept yourself, no one else is going to accept you either. Introverts love to spend time with themselves, and they hate crowds. This is a natural tendency that you cannot change. You cannot expect to wake up one morning and become an exceptional party animal. If you try to do so, it will only result in undue stress and anxiety. It will lead to the development of more problems instead of solving those you already have. Instead of forcing yourself to be outgoing, try to find a middle ground where you feel comfortable and confident.

Accepting your introverted nature can help you focus on the quality of the conversations you have instead of focusing on the number of conversations you have. Remember, the quantity is not as important as the quality.

- **Confidence is Crucial**

You cannot be socially adept if you are not confident. Becoming confident is not a difficult task; you must talk to people and engage them in such a way that they feel heard. You need to appear bold, but not brash. These things will ultimately enhance your social competence. According to research, social competence is great for your self-confidence and your self-perception. You will start to accept yourself during the various social situations you engage if you know how to do it. Practicing social competence is crucial because it will allow you to create new opportunities for yourself. This happens because when you are socially competent, you will approach more and more new people. This way, you will form new contacts, and you will ultimately find new opportunities as well.

Your self-perception plays an important role in how you act in society. If you do not feel self-confident, you will not act confidently. It is necessary to cut out the negativity from your life if you want to be happy, confident, and sociable, which brings us to our next point.

- **Negativity**

If you want to be a positive and sociable person, you need to *stop being negative*. Negative ideas and thoughts are bad for your social, mental, and physical health. When you are not socially confident, you try to find rationales that confirm your negative thoughts. Whenever you feel that you are too negative, stop right there and try to find the evidence supporting the negative thought. Often, you will find nothing, and thus, you will nip the negative thought in the bud.

For instance, if you think that no one likes you because you are boring, stop and find evidence of how you are not boring and how people like you. This will clear all your doubts, and you will feel free once again.

- **Test Your Beliefs**

Once you begin looking for evidence supporting confidence and positivity, you can try testing them. How people react to something does not depend on you; in fact, you cannot control the reactions of other people. If you believe that you are the reason behind certain reactions, then ignore them. How people react solely depends on them. Avoid making any other assumptions.

For instance, if you see a person making a face, you may feel that he or she is teasing you or is bored with you. Sometimes some people end conversations in mid-flow to get up and go away. Don't worry; instead of blaming yourself, try to see whether there were some other reasons why this happened. If a person makes a face while talking to you, it might be because he or she is not comfortable in his or her seat or is not feeling well. If a person ends a conversation abruptly, he or she may have a task that needs to be handled immediately. Or he or she may be an introvert and require some "me" time as soon as possible.

- **Compassion**

If you show compassion toward others, you will receive compassion in return. An exchange of compassion creates a healthy atmosphere conducive to conversation. It can lead to positive interactions that can help to make you more self-confident. It will allow you to understand how to pick up on social cues. It will also help you become more empathetic.

- **Expectations**

When we interact with people, we tend to have expectations regarding some sort of response from them. If you tend to expect a lot from the people or the interaction, you will often end up feeling dissatisfied. This is because you did not have healthy expectations of the interaction. Never take responsibility for how people act around you; that is their decision.

If you are trying to talk to a person and he or she does not respond positively, do not beat yourself up for it. Just shake it off and move on. If a person does not want to talk to you, it is not your problem. It is his or her problem. You cannot be friends with everyone, and not everyone will want to be friends with you. This is perfectly normal.

• Show Interest in Others

A conversation takes place between two or more people. If you only talk about yourself throughout the conversation, no one will be interested in talking to you. You should be able to make your conversation partner comfortable. He or she should feel that you hear and value him or her. This characteristic is known as social competency, and it is an important step in being socially confident. You should try to understand the verbal as well as non-verbal signals and use them to make others feel comfortable. This will help you hone your social skills.

For instance, crossing the arms and avoiding eye contact are two gestures that make people seem uninviting. So, if you want to appear inviting and engaging, avoid using these gestures.

• **Nonverbal Communication**

Introverts do not like to talk, but you can *talk nonverbally* with the help of your body language. Try to adopt a body language that makes you seem more confident. Use body language poses, also known as "power poses", to help you look confident and bold.

There are many different power poses, and a lot of information is available about them online. Adopt a few of them and see the difference for yourself.

Examples:

- Sitting up tall and keeping your chest expanded.
- Placing your hands on the table while sitting on a chair.
- Standing with your shoulders and arms wide open.
- Smiling quite often.
- Making eye contact while talking to people.
- Not fidgeting.
- Clarity of speech.

Along with the gestures and behaviors mentioned above, you can find many more online.

If you can voice your opinions clearly and lucidly, it will make you appear bold and confident. You need to learn how to speak with confidence. Your partner or audience should be able to hear you clearly and understand you properly. Adjust the pitch of your voice. You need to learn how to communicate properly because skillful verbal communication can help you appear comfortable in social gatherings and help people to understand you better.

Mumbling is a sign of low confidence; it also portrays disinterest. It will make people think that you are not comfortable in a conversation.

• **Pace**

Mere clarity of voice cannot help you to be a great speaker; you also need to control and modulate your pace. Your pace should not be too slow or too fast. People should be able to understand you properly. Sometimes, people tend to speak too fast when they are nervous. Speaking too fast will make things difficult for other people, as they will not be able to understand you. To make sure that you are speaking at a normal pace, take steady breaths at regular intervals while speaking. This way, you will be able to control your pace.

If you see that you are speaking too fast, pause for a moment and start speaking slowly once again.

• **Listening Skills**

You can't be a great speaker if you are not a great listener. You need to learn how to listen to people in order to learn how to talk to them. Try to focus on what people are saying. Think about it. This way, you will be able to formulate concrete answers to their questions. You will be able to respond to them appropriately. Your answers need to be thoughtful and calming. If you listen to people while talking, it indicates that you are indeed interested in what they want to say. This will show that you not only care about their ideas and opinions but respect their person as well.

When you are nervous, you tend to pay a lot of attention to yourself. This is natural, but it is still liable to make other people feel uncomfortable. They should not feel that you are not interested in what they are saying.

Do not interrupt people. Instead, let the person finish his or her thought and *then* make your argument.

- **Social Situations**

In the last few tips, we saw how you could become socially confident, but you can't truly be confident until you use these tips in real life. To practice your social confidence skills, you need to put yourself in social settings from time to time. These social situations can help you become more confident and will allow you to practice properly. With time and practice, your social skills will develop, and you will become more and more confident. If you frequently engage yourself in social situations, it will help you become more comfortable in them, and it will reduce your anxiety as well. Instead of putting yourself in only certain kinds of social situations, try to find a variety of social occasions.

Try to initiate conversations. Initiating a conversation is not difficult. You can start with a simple hello, or you can pay a person a compliment and then take the conversation further.

- **Roleplay**

Role-playing really revamps your life if done correctly. Whenever you want to practice your social skills, just ask a friend or a trusted family member to help you. Ask him or her to pretend to be a stranger. Then you can practice your skills with him or her. These practice sessions will help you form an informal script in your head that you can use when you meet real strangers. Just create a simple and flexible format so that you will be able to use it with a lot of people.

- **Friends**

If you find initiating a conversation difficult, don't worry. Just ask a friend to introduce you to people. Meeting friends of your friends is a good way to increase your social circle. You can also practice your communication skills without having to introduce yourself to new people. Ask your friend to introduce you and then take part in the conversation as it naturally unfolds.

• Socialize in New Settings

As we discussed, you need to put yourself in a variety of social settings. Once you get used to a place, you will become comfortable with it. But if you want to enhance your new-found confidence, you need to visit places where no one knows you. This will challenge your self-confidence. If you do not want to be at a crowded party, find a small gathering in which to meet new people. It is recommended that you always be on the lookout for a place to find new and interesting people. This will enhance your confidence immensely.

Small gatherings can be of any sort. For instance, you can find and meet people at a gym, in a book club or hobby club, etc. These places will offer you lots of opportunities to start conversations.

Chapter Twelve: How to Become More Sociable as an Introvert

Introverted people are often considered mysterious, but generally, men face the brunt of being introverted more than women. Men are supposed to display their strength and prowess; they are supposed to take the initiative most of the time. These aspects are crucial for them because they directly affect their personal and professional success. If you are introverted and want to become more sociable for personal or professional reasons, this section will help you do so. It contains various tried and tested tips and methods that will help you become a socially adept introvert in no time. You just need to practice them regularly to make yourself more confident and bolder.

Talking

Many people believe that you need to talk a lot to be sociable. Introverts tend to avoid this, because introverts do not particularly like talking. But don't worry, no one expects you to talk a lot. You just need to calm down and follow the flow of the conversation. When you do need to say something, just say it in a relaxed tone.

Embrace Your Introverted Side

Many people try to change their introverted characteristics because they feel that being introverted is wrong. But this is a myth. Introversion is perfectly natural and normal. Introversion with confidence provides you with a mysterious aura that is irresistible to both genders. You need to learn how to be comfortable in your skin and be confident. Your self-confidence will help you tackle all the awkwardness that is associated with introversion.

Conversation Starters

Nowadays, due to professional and personal commitments, people are likely to meet new people almost every day. This can be nerve-wracking for introverts because they do not like to make small talk. If you are ever stuck in a similar situation, don't worry. Just plan things out beforehand. Instead of meeting a stranger at a random place, choose your places carefully. Your choice should allow you ample conversation topics, so that whenever you sense an awkward silence coming over the conversation, just pick a topic and talk about it. Meeting at a restaurant is a far better option than meeting in a park.

Listen, Think, and Respond

Listening is a great skill that is generally associated with introversion. Introverts love to listen and then think things over. But they rarely respond quickly. If you do not want to scare away your partner, it is recommended to not only listen and think but respond. This will keep the conversation moving forward.

Emphasize Your Strengths

Introverts are born with various skills that are generally known as the characteristics of introversion. Some of these skills include listening, honesty, and great observation skills. If you have some of these skills, be bold about them, and do not hide them. Let them shine brightly. They will surely help you get noticed and ultimately be more sociable.

Practice

Sociable people tend to know what to say, when to say it, and how to say it. Some extroverts are born with this skill, but others learn it with practice. You can learn it, too, by talking to strangers and finding interesting conversation topics. With practice, you, too, will become socially adept.

Entertainer

A great way to become socially accepted is to entertain people. Some people can entertain others without looking silly. If you are not one of these people, then avoid trying to be an entertainer. Introverts rarely feel comfortable being the center of attention. So, instead of forcing yourself into the limelight, stay back and enjoy things from a distance.

Style

Your clothes and style can help you express things that you cannot express verbally. If you find it difficult to talk and express yourself properly through words, let your clothes and accessories speak for you. Upgrading your style is especially recommended if you do not feel confident in your clothes. While being confident in one's skin is necessary, you can expedite the process by being confident in your clothes as well.

Friendliness

Instead of thinking of people as strangers, think of them as friends you only just met. If you treat strangers like friends, you will not feel as awkward. Just use the conversation tactics that you use with your regular friends. This way, you will not be nervous, and you will be able to hold a conversation successfully.

Alone Time

Remember that introversion is normal, and you cannot let go of it. It is your personality, and you need to tap into your introverted side from time to time. You still need to recharge yourself by enjoying some "me" time alone. This time is essential because it will allow you to have fresh ideas.

In summary: to become more sociable, an introvert just needs to become more self-confident. Having self-confidence will automatically boost your social skills. Do not worry a lot about the impressions that you may make on people; just show up, be yourself, and relax.

Chapter Thirteen: How to Network and Make Friends as an Introvert

Finding Someone Who Understands You

Finding people who understand you is difficult. It becomes even more difficult when you are an introvert who loves solitude. Contrary to popular belief, introverts need friends, too. While it is easy to make friends when you are young or are in school, it becomes quite difficult to meet new people and become friends with them when you are an adult. There are many reasons for this; the lack of meeting space, lack of topics of conversation, and lack of time and energy are some reasons why adults find it difficult to make new friends. For introverts, it is even more difficult because they find meeting strangers exhausting.

Introverts tend to be choosy. They cannot be friends with just any random person. They tend to be selective and only try to be friends with people whom they can trust and understand. This is because introverts do not have a lot of social energy, and they do not want to waste it on random people. Extroverts are like large party halls where one can accommodate and entertain a lot of people simultaneously, while introverts are like luxury suites, which means they let only exclusive people enter.

Some people believe that an extrovert can't be close friends with an introvert and vice versa, but this is false. If your friend understands you properly and clicks with you, you will surely appreciate him or her. In this section, let us have a look at some tips that can help you find friends that understand you.

- **Think About Your Acquaintances**

Instead of trying to find new people to be friends with, you can connect with your acquaintances and become friends with them. Everyone has a lot of acquaintances in their life; just check out the ones you find interesting and initiate contact with them. You will make a new friend in no time!

- First Moves

Almost all introverts hate initiating contact. If you are one of these, then you will wait for someone else to talk to you first. This is because you are afraid of rejection. You do not want to get rejected and feel embarrassed or humiliated. This can bring out your self-doubt issues, which in turn can be quite harmful to your mental health. If you have faced a lot of rejection in your life before this, you may not initiate contact with anyone in the future. You feel discouraged and sad. But this discouragement can wreak havoc in your life.

Passivity, especially in adulthood, is problematic. If you act passively in making new contacts, you will find it hard to make new friends in your life. People will never flock to you trying to be your friend; you need to make some effort to contact them. Friendship is a mutual relationship; both parties need to make an equal effort to make it successful. No one will try to become your friend if you do not make any effort. Take matters into your own hands and initiate conversations. Take the first step instead of waiting for others to do so.

- **Masks**

When you meet new people, it is only natural to try to make them feel comfortable. This is especially true for introverted people who want others to like them. But this is a difficult task because you need to maintain an aura of happiness all the time to do so. It takes a lot of work to do this, and ultimately it will not produce any significant results.

You cannot be friends with someone if you are not "real," and to appeal to someone, people tend to hide their quirks and negative aspects, putting forward only their positive side. They literally create a façade, and everyone knows that keeping up a façade for a long time is not only difficult but impossible. You will soon start to hate your friends because the facade will make you miserable. It will suck up your energy and will leave you feeling tired and empty.

So, instead of creating a façade just so that people can like you, try to present your true self. Be confident about yourself and don't worry if people don't appreciate you in the beginning. Your vulnerability will allow you to connect with other people effectively.

- **Ask Questions**

Two things are almost givens in this world: people love talking about themselves, and introverts like listening and contemplating. You can use these two factors to your advantage. Whenever you meet new people, talk a few minutes about yourself and then ask questions about them. They will surely appreciate your interest in them, and you will be able to conduct a successful conversation. Use your listening skills to cover your weak verbal skills.

- **Notice How You Feel**

This is a great way to test whether you enjoy hanging out with your new friend or not. When you hang out with the friend, do you feel incredibly tired, or do you feel happy, and perhaps energized? As an introvert, it is perfectly natural to feel kind of tired after spending time with a new person, but this tiredness is often pleasing. If you feel excessively tired and uncomfortable, then perhaps the new friendship is not meant to be.

Emotionally needy people generally seek introverts to display their emotional baggage. As introverts are good listeners, emotionally needy people tend to use them as sounding boards, or, sometimes, a metaphorical punching bag. Introverts, who prefer others to initiate contact, are generally happy in this relationship in the beginning, but with time, they realize that they are not really friends with the person. If you are ever caught in a similar situation, it is recommended you back away gradually and break ties with him or her gently. You do not want relationships that drain you.

- **Awkwardness**

Many introverts tend to stay away from people because they feel awkward around others. Even when they meet new people, they keep their positive characteristics, such as a fun personality or quirkiness, hidden. Their true selves only come out when they feel comfortable with the person. But this way you may miss the chance to meet new people.

Don't worry if you feel awkward with a person in the beginning: in time you will become more comfortable and will start enjoying your friend's company.

- **Meetups**

You cannot be friends with a person if you do not hang out with each other from time to time; ask your friend to meet you and hang out with you at least once a week. A simple lunch on the weekends will suffice. You can also go for a group hangout so that you will be able to meet new people. It is recommended to schedule hangout sessions; in this way, you will be able to form a routine. *Introverts love routines.*

- **Go Slowly**

Friendships do not happen overnight, especially in the case of adults. It takes time for a relationship to mature and develop properly. Do not try to force a friendship. Let it develop gradually; a gradually developed friendship will always be better than a simple, overnight relationship.

Remember, the quality of friends is more important than the number of friends. It is better to have a small circle of extremely close and trustworthy friends than to have a lot of shallow acquaintances.

Making Friends in the Modern World

Introverted people find it quite difficult to make new friends, especially when they are forced to do so. It can be quite an exhausting experience. In the last section, we saw how an introvert could make new friends. Many other ways can help you to become friends with people. Modern amenities can make it easier to make new friends. Finding friends on the Internet has become quite easy but becoming friends in real life with your online friends can be quite difficult. In this section, let us have a look at how you can use online methods to make online friends and turn them into friends in real life as well.

- **Blog Posts**

Blogs are a great way to express yourself and present your ideas to the world. A lot of people read blogs frequently, though only a few people comment on them. Blogs are not meant to be a form of a one-way conversation. You can contact the blog writer and show your appreciation of him or her by commenting on positive things about their blog. You can also use this method to find and make new friends. Just by reading the blogs and commenting on them, you can form positive relationships. You can then continue those friendships in the form of emails and social media.

Some people tend to use blogs as a sounding board where they just put their ideas. They do not want any comments or replies to their content. But most blog writers appreciate it when people comment on their blogs and compliment their hard work. If you frequently comment on particular blogs, you will ultimately form a strong bond with the writer.

- **Join Facebook Groups**

Facebook groups have become a great way to meet people who think alike and like the same things. Finding new friends is quite easy on social media. It is easy to become friends with likeminded people. Join some groups related to things you are interested in. For instance, a reading group, a cooking group, or a movie group can help you make friends with ease. Just post your experiences in the group and comment on the experiences of others. Show that you are genuinely interested in talking to people and interacting with them.

Many people have found lifelong friends with the help of Facebook and other social media sites and apps. There are many groups on Facebook that are especially great for introverts. Just search for them on the site and enjoy making new friends.

- **Tweet People**

Another great way to meet new people and talk to them online is Twitter. Twitter may be quite daunting, especially in the beginning, because it moves quickly, and there is a text limit. The concept of DMs can be quite confusing. Still, Twitter is a great way to connect with people if you are an introvert.

Twitter is especially great for an introvert because it allows you to listen without having to talk to people. As made sufficiently clear before, introverts love listening. Twitter can allow you to listen to people by "following" them. You can stay up to date with people without having to talk to them all the time. You can also physically meet the people that you met on Twitter. This way, you will be able to find some "real" friends easily.

- **Twitter Chats**

Once you understand how "following" and "lists" work on Twitter, you can begin to use other options. For instance, Twitter can be used to have some meaningful interactions and can also help you to build great relationships. To do this, you can use the Twitter chat option to meet new people and talk to them.

Twitter chats are comparatively more regular than meeting people in bars. You can meet the same person over and over and form a great relationship with him or her. If you find it difficult to handle Twitter chat on your mobile device, drop it and just use your computer. The interface is much better on the computer than on mobile devices.

- **Setup Skype Dates**

Video conferencing platforms such as Google Hangouts, Skype, and Zoom are great services with which to meet and talk to new people. These services can allow you to be in your comfort zone and meet new people without any problem. You can sit in your home office or your bedroom and talk to people from all over the world.

You can literally be sitting in one corner of the U.S. and talking to a person sitting in Indonesia.

Skype and videoconferences are great ways to contact people. You can also have a one-on-one chat with friends from another part of the world.

- **Hire Them**

Another way to meet new people and become friends with them is by hiring them. If you have a small business, you can hire new employees and become friends with them. This option is not always feasible, as people do not work for free. So, whenever you need a new employee, you will, of course, have to spend some amount of money for their services. But if you can hire some people, then it will be a great experience as you will be able to form a strong bond with them.

If you do not have a business of your own, you can become friends with your colleagues at work. Gone are the days when people used to think that it was a bad decision to be friends with your colleagues. Get out and become friends with them!

- **Ask for Intros**

This is another great way to make new friends. If you want to be friends with someone, but you do not know them, then you can ask a mutual friend to introduce you. People love helping other people because it makes them feel important. If you ask someone politely to introduce you to someone else, he or she will be glad to do so.

You can do this frequently to make new friends. Even if you do not end up being friends with the person, you can still add him or her as a contact. It will certainly pay off in the long term. Asking someone to introduce you to someone else will allow you to form a close bond with the first person as well. This method can yield doubled results.

- **Attend Conferences**

If you are finished meeting people online and now want to meet people physically, there are many new methods to do so. Gone are the days when you could only meet people in bars and clubs. Now you can meet and make friends with people anywhere. Every month, there are many different conferences and conventions happening. Just find some conventions that you find interesting and attend them. Here you will be able to find new people and talk to them. This is a great way to make new friends and perhaps get in touch with your old friends as well, finding them there because you have mutual interests.

• **Introduce Others**

If you cannot find someone to introduce you to a person, you can introduce other people to other individuals. So, if you feel that two people should know each other because they will enjoy being friends, just introduce them. You will act as a sort of friendship matchmaker. This way, you will be able to connect with a lot of people and will be able to form strong bonds with them. When you connect with other people, they connect with you as well. Thus, you end up making new friends from all directions.

So, instead of making excuses, get up and get out of your house (or not) and try to make new friends. If you do not make an effort, you will not be able to make new friends. Use the modern amenities mentioned in this book to help you tackle the world of adult friendship. Don't worry; with ample time and patience, you will be able to forge strong lifelong bonds without any problem.

Chapter Fourteen: Introverts in Professional Settings

Introverts who work in offices tend to be surrounded by colleagues and employees throughout the day. People tend to exchange stories, make acquaintances, make friends, form contacts, etc. It is recommended that you join the conversation and become friends with other people. These contacts are crucial if you want to climb the ladder of success. But most introverts cannot do this, as they are afraid to approach strangers and talk to them.

Around one third or more of the people you meet are introverts. These people prefer intimate settings and events as opposed to the larger gathering enjoyed by extroverts. They do not like excessively stimulating and loud atmospheres. But generally, society is more involved with and aligned toward extroverts. This is especially true in the professional world where introverts are treated as second-rate citizens.

But it does not matter. You need to strive and work hard if you want to succeed in the corporate world, especially if you are an introvert. You need to work hard at getting to know your colleagues. In this section, let's consider some tips that can help you become successful in a professional setting.

Be Yourself

While this may sound like a cliché, it is still true. You cannot succeed if you are not true to yourself. Beating yourself up every day just because you are not an extrovert will not take you anywhere; rather, it leads to the development of more and more problems. While it is true that having certain extroverted characteristics can help you immensely in the world, expecting yourself to behave and act just like extroverts is illogical and childish. Instead of doing this, try to make your introverted personality stand out.

If you do not feel comfortable in crowds and prefer small groups, then don't beat yourself up about it. There is nothing wrong with feeling more comfortable in a small group. You need to understand your characteristics and use them as your assets. For instance, introverts are blessed with great thinking and listening skills. You can use these to form good, intimate, long-lasting relationships with people. Just focus on things that matter and ignore the ones that do not.

Redefine Your Approach

Try to redefine your approach toward life and your career. If you avoid meeting people because you hate crowds, try to meet them in more intimate settings. Arrange your meetings in smaller offices or cafes. You can also conduct meetings at golf courses or tennis courts. Just find a place that you find intimate and comfortable. This way, you will be able to talk to your partner without any inhibitions.

Focus on Remarkability

According to many studies, our brains are well suited to respond to new and interesting situations. This means that if the situation is new, you can make exciting memories. So, if you want to meet new people but are scared or nervous about it, make the meeting exciting by incorporating something new into it. For instance, if you own a farm, conduct the meeting *on the farm*. Try some new activities to make things exciting and memorable.

Take Baby Steps

If approaching people and initiating conversations scare you, don't worry. Just take baby steps and move on slowly. Always try to step out of your complacent zone slowly, one step at a time.

Start with a safety net. Start the conversation and move on slowly. If you find the experience intimidating, don't worry; keep on practicing, and move forward.

Take Advantage of The Winner Effect

The "winner effect" means that whenever a person wins, their body receives a pleasant shock from the brain. This pleasant shock is great because it quickly boosts your confidence for a while. The more you win, the better your confidence levels will be. So, whenever you plan to meet new people, try to win at something.

Tell Yourself the Right Things

Recontextualize things. When you are scared about things, try to think about them from a positive point of view. This can help you enhance your performance. For instance, if you hate speaking and generally get nervous about meetings, do not talk a lot; instead, listen and make some interesting and skillful comments. This way, you will be able to participate in the conversation without feeling flustered. You won't have to do small talk either!

Ask for a Warm Introduction

If you want to make a connection at a social event but are scared to do so, don't worry. Just ask a friend to introduce you to someone. Initiating a conversation can be difficult, which is why many introverts fail to make the effort. Instead of making the necessary effort, introverts tend to sit back in a corner and not talk to people at all. Instead of doing this, explain the situation to a friend and ask him or her to introduce you. This way, you will be able to talk to the person and make a new contact without facing any severe emotional discomfort.

If All Else Fails, Outsource

If you have tried all the options above but have still failed, don't worry; there are other options that you can try. A simple way to connect with people is by asking people to introduce you to others. Ask a friend or a colleague to be a matchmaker for you. This way, you can connect to the person and your friend as well.

It does not matter whether you are an extrovert or an introvert. Anyone can find good, close, and life-long friends, guides, mentors, and influencers through others, but it takes effort. Try these tips to find out which ones suit you the most; they will surely help you become more comfortable around people, and you will be making new friends in no time.

Chapter Fifteen: Tips for Maintaining Relationships

Relationships are exciting, but they can be difficult. They are especially scary for introverts who do not know how to initiate contact. Introverts feel multiple emotions when they try to initiate romantic contacts. While extroverts only feel the giddiness and butterflies-in-the-stomach feeling associated with love, introverts may feel nervousness, fear, and anxiety. The thought of getting into a relationship is enthralling, but it can also be embarrassing, scary, and strange for introverts.

Most introverts want to have a strong and close romantic relationship, but they are generally uncertain about how to go about it. Some introverts believe that dating can only work for them if they can find their soulmate. Due to this hunt for the perfect soulmate, they tend to miss out on many good opportunities to meet excellent people. Introverts can surely find some great people if they start to come out of their shells and make some effort.

In this section, let us have a look at some common tips that can help you achieve a great relationship.

Remove Your Inhibitions

If you like someone and want to go out with them, do not confuse yourself with a gaggle of questions. Just be bold and simply *ask them out immediately*. Generally, when you are an introvert, you tend to think a lot about your prospective date. You are scared about it because you do not know whether it will work out or not. If you do think that it will work, you tend to concentrate on how it will become the best relationship in your life. This amount of fantasizing will only lead to the development of major problems. Introverts love to analyze the past and dream about the future, but many times this makes them ignore the present. Avoid doing this.

Go One Step at a Time

Introverts tend to think a lot before taking serious steps, and in the case of relationships, this may slow the process because of their tendency to daydream. Introverts tend to dream a lot about the future of their relationship. While some amount of fantasizing is okay, try to keep it limited. Instead of dreaming of spending your whole lives together, try to get to know your date better. Understand his or her likes, hobbies, dislikes, goals, work, family, education, friends, etc. Check whether your wavelengths match with each other or not. Avoid jumping to positive or negative conclusions. Reflect on your feelings and think about them carefully. Use your introvert's powers of thinking.

Build the Rapport

It is crucial to build a good rapport with the person you are trying to date. Instead of focusing on yourself, try to focus on your date. Understand their feelings, emotions, and thoughts. While thinking about the date, try to find out your date's ideas about you. Introverts generally tend to *detach from* and *attach to* people too soon. Try to maintain a balance, or your relationship will suffer.

Tell Them What You Are Like

Introverts can be confusing to many people. If your date does not understand you, he or she may think that you are moody and dull. In such a case, it is better to be honest, and tell your date how and what you feel. Let them know how solitude is crucial for you and how you need the vigor you get from isolation. Your date should know the future of your relationship. If your date understands your needs, then great! If not, it is better to move on right away.

Talk about Things That Are Important to You

Introverts and extroverts consider things differently. For instance, the perceptions and values that introverts hold are different from the perceptions and values that extroverts possess. If you are an introvert who is dating an extrovert, sit down and discuss what things are important for both of you individually and as a couple. Sharing and being honest in a relationship is essential.

It does not have to be extremely personal. You can share simple needs such as how you like small crowds and quiet places. This way, your partner will understand your needs properly.

Demonstrate Your Strengths

If you are operating under the notion that introverts are disliked all over the world, then drop it immediately! This is a false notion that has been perpetuated by inconsiderate stereotypes. People love introverts as much as they do extroverts. Instead of hiding your characteristics, display them. Wear them on your sleeve with pride. Use your characteristics and make them your strengths. This way, you will be true to yourself and will be able to make your relationship successful.

Chapter Sixteen: Tips on Developing Strong Relationships

In the previous chapter, we covered how difficult it is for introverts to get into relationships and maintain them; because the world is largely focused on extroverts and their needs and desires, introverts generally do not get enough attention. They are not talked about a lot, either. This is typical of all walks of life, be it professional or personal.

If you find it difficult to get into or maintain a relationship because you are an introvert, don't worry. Use these tricks along with the tips mentioned in the previous chapter to come out of your shell. These tips will surely help you to develop a good relationship.

- **Meaningful Conversations**

Liking your partner for superficial reasons will lead to catastrophic results. This is because a relationship cannot survive just based on superficial likes and dislikes. If you want a relationship to work, you need to understand the theories and possibilities of it. You should be able to form a deep and close bond with the person. Introverts love to think and talk about ideas. They prefer to talk a lot about things that they love. They do not care for single-word answers if the topic is interesting. While the term has received much flak over the past few years, it is true; introverts are "sapiosexual". They love people who are cultured and intelligent. They like to be with people who are timeless, aware, and classy.

They would rather be with people who are good conversationalists than those who are into superficial things alone. They do not like smooth talkers, and they would rather have someone challenge them intellectually. Introverts love it when people ask them thought-provoking questions.

• **Less Stimulating Environments**

The brains of introverts get stimulated easily. This means that they do not need a lot of stimulating situations to become happy and achieve pleasure. Introverts do not need to go to exciting parties or large gatherings to feel happy. They hate places where they need to shout just to get their ideas heard in public.

If you are an introvert who finds dating difficult, sit down and try to find the reasons behind it. Many times, introverts avoid dating because dating entails going out of the house and meeting people in noisy and crowded places such as bars and clubs. These places can be overwhelming for you. They will also exhaust you quickly, and you will end up feeling sad and desolate.

If you want to enjoy your date, visit a far less crowded area. As a person who gets overwhelmed easily, it can be quite daunting to visit a heavily crowded event or places such as a theme park or a concert. Instead of going to places like this, try to visit other, quieter, and more serene places. For instance, instead of picking a club as your date venue, go to a small café. Instead of visiting that popular buffet place, why not go to a small, relatively unknown restaurant where the food is delicious, and the ambiance is peaceful? The venues of your dates are quite important because they allow you to study your potential partner. They allow you to understand his or her personality, and they make you feel comfortable and relaxed. A person who is relaxed and comfortable thinks more clearly than a person who is anxious and scared.

- **Slow and Steady**

Introverts like to take things slowly. You would rather go on multiple dates before choosing a partner. You prefer to collect information about your date and understand their motives, life goals, and personality. You rarely display affection toward someone if you do not understand them and know them thoroughly. It may make you seem strange in the beginning, but that does not matter; with ample self-control and patience, you can enjoy a date properly. Remember, a relationship cannot survive if it is only based on superficial things; you must see what lies at the core of the relationship, *and your date.* Inform your date that you prefer to take things slowly, and then watch their reaction. If they seem to be okay with it, great! If not, adjust your priorities slightly.

- **Sensitivity**

Introverts are sensitive, and they like sensitive people. If your partner is not sensitive to your needs and desires, then your relationship will not survive. Don't bottle up your emotions, because they will eventually explode! You need to find a person who is equally sensitive to you. This does not mean that you should look only for an introvert, as many extroverts can be quite sensitive as well. While introverts do not mind conflict, they would rather stay away from it. If you and your date fight a lot, sit down and contemplate that.

- **Get Out of Your Head**

Introverts tend to overthink and overanalyze a lot. It is difficult for them to be in the moment, especially when their mind jumps from one point to the next. It is a natural phenomenon and is a part of being an introvert. If your date finds it silly, let them know why you are this way; he or she will understand. Most of the time, when you are not in the moment, you are perhaps thinking of what to say next or what should be your next move. This is important because it allows you to control the future of your relationship. You don't want it to fail. By looking at the relationship from various points of view, you can prevent that from happening.

- **Read Between the Lines**

Introverts like to read between the lines because it reveals things that the conversation does not. Introverts are born with great thinking and observation skills and are highly focused on things that they like. They are subtle and not brash. Use your powers to understand your date, noticing the nuances of the conversation. Notice the body language and gestures, pay close attention to what your date says and the way they say it. Even the smallest cues can help you understand whether there is some future to this relationship or not. If you ever feel that nothing can be done about this relationship or if you see some red flags, move on and find someone better. If you find a person problematic in the first meeting, you are bound to find them problematic in all your future meetings. So instead of giving people the benefit of the doubt, just move on.

- **Need for Space**

Introverts need a lot of space and time to think things over. You need solitude to think about matters. This solitude is essential because it allows you to recharge your energy. Without energy, you cannot date people properly as you cannot skillfully answer or ask questions. Your date must understand that you need your solitude from time to time. If you find your date to be too suffocating or overbearing, it is better to break things off immediately. A suffocating relationship will make you suffer, and it will make you hide deep within your shell. If you ever feel that your data is being overbearing, let them know. If they try to change their behavior, all is good, but if they don't, then move on.

- **Quality Time**

No matter how many hours you spend together, if you do not find it interesting, you will probably never go on another date with him/her. For introverts, quality matters more than quantity. If you like a person and you go on a date with him or her, only to realize that they have nothing good to say, move on. You will not be able to spend quality time with this person, and you will surely suffer in the long term. You need to gain something from a conversation, as mindless small talk will take you nowhere. If your date cannot keep you interested, even for a few minutes, there is no future to this relationship anyway. It is better to move on now than to create a scene later.

 • **Be Yourself**

We live in a world that is obsessed with self-improvement. Everyone is trying to improve all the time and work toward their own betterment. While it is commendable to work on self-improvement, it is necessary to check what things come under the umbrella term of "self-improvement." For instance, introverts are often forced to adopt the characteristics of extroverts because people believe that these characteristics are better than the ones that introverts have. Since their childhood, introverts are forced to be conditioned and molded in such a way that they end up being a faux extrovert. As mentioned already, this is impossible; introverts cannot become extroverts or vice versa. This dehumanizing process should be stopped immediately. If you, as a child, went through such trauma, it is possible that you may still be suffering from it. It is okay, but do not take your baggage everywhere you go; try to adjust your orientation and tackle it as a problem instead.

Instead of trying to appease your date by showing how extroverted you are, accept your true self and be who you are. Do not hide your true colors. Be bold and beautiful and let the flag of introversion fly.

 • **Don't Assume Anything**

Do not assume anything when you date someone. Use your introvert's instincts; sit down and relax, thinking and mulling over your ideas. Silence can be quite confusing to extroverts, so let them know that you like silence and that it does not mean anything negative. You should allow your date to understand that you are an introvert and that you look at the world from a different point of view. Do not presume that your date will be ready to adjust to you. Many extroverts and, in fact, many introverts, do not know how to deal with introverts. That is perfectly okay, because the world is centered on extroverts. So, instead of forcing your date to try to understand you, or falsely assuming that they understand you already, try to let them know the nature of your personality. This is not a form of warning. Rather, it is being bold and confident about your true self. Remember, no one will accept you if you do not accept yourself.

Chapter Seventeen: How to Optimize Your Introvert Superpower

Every person with every personality type is born with particular traits and characteristics that can either hinder their progress or help it. Introverts have various characteristics that are often looked down upon in today's world. But instead of ignoring these characteristics, you can use them and modify them in such a way that they can help you in achieving your goals. In this chapter, let us have a look at how your introverted characteristics can help you in your day-to-day life.

Introverts and Career Options

Finding a good career option is often difficult for introverts because of the various characteristics and traits they possess. Introversion is not a single concept; rather, it is a compilation of various personality and emotional traits that are present or absent in people to varying degrees. This makes the task of understanding introverts quite complex. Introversion can be divided into various categories, but the most common categories that we have already discussed are social, thinking, anxious, or inhibited. To choose a career, first, find out what kind of introvert you are.

In this section, you will find a long list of various career options that are suitable for introverts. For the convenience of the reader, these career options are divided according to the types of introversion mentioned above. Do remember that these types tend to overlap a lot, and no one can say for sure that they belong to only one of the above types. So, you should select career options according to your personality style.

Gone are the days when people used to believe that introverts were only good for certain low-paying jobs. Now people know that introverts can prove to be an asset if you know how to use them. The variety of career options given in this section proves the fact that introverts have a lot of career options in which they can perform well with ease.

Remember that this section is meant for reading only. It is always recommended to contact a career counselor before picking any of the following careers as your permanent job. This way, you will be able to understand whether you are really meant for the job or not.

Social Introvert Jobs

Social introversion sounds quite paradoxical because introverts are well known for avoiding social settings. While it may sound dubious or conflicting, this term refers to introverts who do not like getting into social situations and who like to live and think in solitude. It is a well-known fact that introverts love solitude because solitude allows them to recharge and refresh. If they cannot find "alone time", they would rather be with a small group of people instead of being stuck with a large crowd.

It should be noted that the introverts who fall into this category face little or no social anxiety; they merely lean toward finding smaller social gatherings where they won't have to interact with a lot of people.

Social introverts are known to be quite loyal. They understand their own boundaries as well as others'. They would rather develop strong relationships with people instead of attacking or ignoring them. Introverts rarely accept new friends in their social circle. But if the person becomes a part of the inner circle, he or she will never feel alone again; introverts love to take care of their friends.

Social introverts are quite complex, which is why there are a lot of work options available.

If you are a social introvert, pay close attention to the nature of your potential future work environments. A lot of people who are social introverts tend to prefer working from home or similar spaces. Most social introverts try to avoid workplaces that are too noisy, crowded, or full. They would never choose to work in a place that does not offer them privacy. But your career does not depend upon these factors a lot. You can enjoy most of these factors in a lot of different careers if your employer understands your needs.

But there exist many careers in which you do not need to interact with a lot of people anyway. Many of these careers include various trades and skill-based occupations. Let us have a look at some good career options for social introverts.

- **Database Administrator**

These people are responsible for handling data in big firms, industries, and offices. It is a good-paying job.

- **Private Chef**

The nature of this job depends on where you decide to work. For instance, if you are a private chef to a billionaire, you will be paid well to make exotic food for a single individual or family, with only an occasional party of varying size.

- **Electrical or Electronic Engineering Technician**

You do not have to talk to a lot of people in this job, and spend a lot of time exercising your penchant for precise thinking and problem solving.

- **Mechanical Drafter**

This is a great option for people who are artistically inclined and detail oriented.

- **Civil or architectural drafter**

This is great for people who are good at management and planning. It is also a satisfying option for introverts who are into culture and art.

- **Plumber**

Plumbing does not involve a lot of talking to strangers. It is a great job option for people who like to fix things.

- **Commercial driver**

While drivers, especially commercial drivers, must face a lot of strangers every day, it does not matter because you do not have to interact with them.

- **Industrial machinery mechanic**

Industrial machinery mechanics do not need to interact with a lot of people, and they can often choose their work hours.

- **Heavy equipment mechanic**

Like industrial machinery mechanics, heavy equipment mechanics do not need to meet a lot of people, and they can work under their own terms.

- **Private investigator**

Being a P.I. (private investigator) was once one of the most glamorous of occupations. A P.I. can work alone and investigate without having a partner or employees.

- **HVAC mechanic**

HVAC mechanics enjoy work environments much like those of heavy equipment and industrial machinery mechanics.

- **Interpreter or translator**

Translation involves thinking and precision. You can be a verbal translator, or if you do not like speaking with and meeting people, you can translate written works.

- **Carpenter**

Carpenters earn well, and if you love woodworking you can convert your hobby into a profession.

- Heavy tractor-trailer truck driver

Truck drivers generally travel alone. You can pick up other hobbies while doing this job and still enjoying the solitude that you desire.

- **Motorboat mechanic**

This job, too, provides a lot of privacy and peace.

- **Welder**

This job is great for introverts who love peace and solitude.

- **Dental lab technician**

While this does involve meeting people, you can avoid them by concentrating on your work.

- **Motorcycle mechanic**

This is a great option for introverts who are skilled with their hands.

- **Small engine mechanic**

This is a great job option for introverts who like machines.

- **Animal trainer**

Introverts generally love spending time with animals more than humans. This is because animals cannot speak and are never judgmental.

- **Baker**

Baking is an art involving precision, thinking, and passion. If you are a great baker, why not turn your hobby into a career?

Thinking Introvert Careers

Unlike social introverts, thinking introverts do not mind social engagement. While they do not go out of their way to meet people, they don't particularly mind meeting them, either. Their energy levels do not deplete quickly after meeting other people. A major characteristic of thinking introverts is that they are highly introspective and thoughtful.

Thinking introverts have highly developed imagination and a sense of creativity. They are generally the first person to think outside the box. They can see the big picture and can bring out new ideas and innovations. Many thinking introverts are known to be good listeners. They don't just listen, but they respect other people's ideas as well. It is no wonder that thinking introverts are commonly seen in fields such as technology, engineering, art, design, etc. Some great careers for *thinking introverts* include:

- **Aerospace engineer**

This fits well for people who like to build new things and think up new ideas.

- **Environmental engineer**

This is a good option for thinking introverts who want to be innovative.

- **Industrial engineer**

This is a good option for thinking introverts who like to be bold and creative.

- **Civil engineer**

If you like planning and precision, this is a good option for you.

- **Computer programmer**

Programming needs a lot of patience and thinking. This is a highly suitable job for thinking introverts.

- **Web developer**

Like programming, web development needs a lot of patience and thinking, as well as creativity.

- **Video game artist**

If you are creative and good with art, you will reach new heights in this career field.

- **Fashion designer**

This is perfect for people who want to create new things to show off their talents.

- **Interior designer**

These people need good listening skills and patience.

- **Graphic designer**

This is a very lucrative job for introverts, as you can enjoy your privacy while working.

Anxious Introvert Jobs

Anxious introverts are like social introverts who prefer to be alone. But unlike social introverts, this desire to be alone comes from anxiety about other people and their perceptions about you. Anxious introverts are generally shy and awkward, especially in a social situation. They tend to worry a lot about their past and their future, which makes them ignore their present.

Some people may even feel weak and crippled due to their social anxiety. While there are many negatives associated with this type of introversion, there are many positives about it as well. Anxious introverts are extremely detail-oriented and love planning and precision. They are also highly focused. This makes them suitable for many different careers that call for precision, focus, and planning.

Many career options for this category include jobs that need a lot of planning and critical work. These jobs tend to be highly detail-oriented, and many involve saving people's lives. Here is a list of some of the career options that anxious introverts can take up:

- **Statistician**

Being a statistician involves a lot of precise calculations that can be difficult for others to understand.

- **Commercial pilot**

Being a commercial pilot requires immense patience and attention to detail. One wrong move can result in the deaths of hundreds of people.

- **Technical writer**

Technical writers need to be able to muster a lot of attention to avoid mistakes. This job also provides anxious introverts their much-desired solitude.

- **Accountant or auditor**

Like statisticians, these jobs need the precision required for accurate calculations.

- **Medical lab technician or technologist**

A medical lab technician needs to pay a lot of attention to the details, which is why this is a great job for anxious introverts.

- **Aircraft mechanic**

Being an aircraft mechanic requires a lot of attention to detail. It is good for people who can focus.

- Audio engineering technician

This requires the precision necessary for making minute adjustments.

- **Auto mechanic**

This requires intense precision and attention to detail.

- **Proofreader**

Reading, finding errors, and rectifying them takes a lot of focus and protracted attention. This is a great job for people who want to work in privacy.

Inhibited Introvert Careers

Inhibited introverts generally appear laid-back and very reserved. They tend to do things at their own pace. They do not like to speak or react immediately and prefer to think before they answer. They avoid making rash decisions and taking action before analysis. Inhibited introverts do not like to do anything without thinking about it a lot beforehand.

Their reserved nature and immense thinking capabilities allow these introverts to reflect upon things deeply. It also provides them a lot of observation skills and allows them to look at the big picture. Therefore, these introverts tend to do well at jobs that allow them to be the *voice of reason.*

Inhibited introverts love to think about difficult choices and questions. They do not mind big challenges, and they handle them with confidence. Ergo, many inhibited introverts work well in fields such as counseling, science, and various vocational areas. All these areas need critical thinking. Here is a list of some common career options for inhibited introverts:

- **Physicist**

Physicists need a lot of critical thinking and precision in pursuing ideas and extrapolating indicators from data.

- **Astronomer**

A great opportunity for detail-oriented introverts who like to think a lot while being alone.

- **Geoscientist**

Being a geoscientist requires a lot of research and thinking.

- **Personal financial advisor**

While it involves a certain degree of interpersonal communication, it is still recommended for an inhibited introvert.

- **Biochemist or biophysicist**

Like physicists, this job requires a lot of precise thinking.

- **Management analyst**

Management analysts must pay a lot of attention to detail and possess creativity.

- **Microbiologist**

A lot of research and precision goes into being a microbiologist.

- **Market research analyst or marketing specialist**

Understanding and predicting the trends of the market needs a lot of focused thinking.

- **Anthropologist or archaeologist**

Both fields require a lot of research and thinking.

- **Conservation scientist**

This requires a lot of focus.

- **Creative or non-fiction writer**

Writing entails a lot of thinking, creativity, and focus.

- **Wildlife biologist**

A love for animals and solitude will allow you to succeed in this career.

- **Career or education counselor**

Analyzes the life decisions of a person in a focused and precise manner.

- **Marriage or Family Therapist**

Analyzes the intricate details of marriage and the married life of the couple.

- **Mental health counselor**

These counselors must remember much detail in order to help others properly.

- **Addictions counselor**

Being an addictions counselor requires a lot of thinking and focus on helping people.

Chapter Eighteen: The Introverted Leader

Why Introverts Make Great Leaders

For decades, people have believed that introverts cannot be great and capable leaders because they do not possess those qualities needed for leadership. People believed that introverts are incapable and ineffective, and their possessing a leadership style is just not plausible.

This myth has percolated to the top of the business world. In fact, more than 65% of senior executives in the western world believe that introversion is a bad sign for business-oriented teammates. They believe that only 6% of introverts can take over huge companies and manage a team successfully. Many businessmen believe that leaders need to possess certain qualities such as gregariousness, outgoing nature, and expert networking skills to be successful. As these skills are generally perceived to be inherent in extroverts and generally lacking in introverts, many leaders dismiss introverts out-of-hand when considering candidates for leadership positions. This is obviously a myth and a nonsensical position.

What Is an Introvert?

Introverts and extroverts, as terms, were first introduced by Carl Jung in the 1920s. Introverts are people who tend to get their energy from time spent alone rather than in socializing. Extroverts tend to get their energy from socializing. Introverts are generally introspective and quiet. They are often observant, but sometimes shy.

Some people believe that introverts and extroverts are like opposite poles and that there is a wide difference between the two types, but this is not true; true introverts and true extroverts do not exist. People tend to be somewhere towards the middle of the spectrum in both these personality types.

Introverts are often written off as antisocial people who do not like talking to people or being around them. This is, of course, false. Introverts are not necessarily anti-social. They prefer solitude because they like to contemplate and think over matters that are important to them. They feel rejuvenated and refreshed when they have time alone, allowing them to look at things from a new and different perspective. Many people hold to the myth that being an introvert means that you are a loser and that you are an awkward nerd. But this is a myth; introverts *do* like to spend time with other people – just on *their own terms.*

As said above, no one is thoroughly extroverted or introverted. But according to an estimate, around 33-55% of people are skewed towards introversion. But this demographic changes drastically once we enter the world of business. In the corporate world, more than 96% of people are extroverted. The number is even higher when the topmost positions are considered as a category, showing that there is a strong prejudice against introverts in the world of business. Many leaders rank extroversion as the best trait that a leader can have. This bias against introversion is not only harmful to introverts, but it also harmful to the business world itself. Due to this bias, the world of business has lost countless great leaders who could have changed the world!

While it is now generally accepted that there is a bias against introverts in the world of business, the question is, what is the reason behind this bias? To find the answer to the problem, let's consider the history behind it.

How Culture Defines "Leadership"

The definitions of "leader" and "leadership" vary, but in simple cultural terms, leadership is the process through which other people are influenced in such a way that they work together to achieve a common goal of the group.

In the beginning, leaders were meant to be people who encouraged their team members to work collectively toward the team goals. But with time, the definition changed, and now leaders are singular, charismatic, bold titans who rule their teams. In this paradigm, the leader's team-building skills are not as important as managing the team's public image.

There are dozens of studies throughout the last century aimed at finding out what traits make good leaders. If the results of these tests and studies are taken cumulatively, the traits mentioned in the studies are present in both personality types, and some are perhaps seen more in introverts than extroverts. None of the traits go against the typical behavior and attitude of introverts, so it is a curious case as to why introverts are still not being offered leadership positions. The answer to this problem is perhaps the myths that surround introversion and leadership. Let us have a look at these myths one by one.

- **Myth #1: Introverts do not like leadership roles**

This is one of the most perpetuated myths about introverts, and it is clearly false. Introverts do want to be leaders; *they just do not get the chance to do so.*

Introverts are present and have succeeded in almost all walks of life, be it sports, arts, business, movies, music, or politics. Many famous leaders in these fields who were introverts include Audrey Hepburn, Michael Jordan, Mahatma Gandhi, and Albert Einstein. Many important presidents of the United States of America, including Abraham Lincoln, Thomas Jefferson, and Barack Obama, were introverts. Even in the world of business, many prominent leaders, including Mark Zuckerberg, Bill Gates, and Warren Buffet, are introverts. This proves that introverts are present and successful at leading in all fields.

Introverts can do well in any field; they just need to learn how to use their skills properly. Instead of keeping their talents and skills hidden, introverts should tap into them. Many introverted traits that are generally looked down upon in the world of business can prove to be beneficial.

- **Myth #2: Introverts don't have the "people skills"**

Another myth that is popular in the world of business is that introverts do not possess "people skills". This means that they do not possess the skills such as confidence and charisma that are necessary for effective leadership.

Recent research found that while it is indeed more likely that a charming individual will be hired as a CEO, his or her charm does not guarantee his or her success and performance. This means that charm has nothing to do with performance. In the same study, it was observed that introverted leaders did far better than leaders who were hired just for their charming personalities.

It is true that introverted leaders are generally not as cheerful or bubbly as an extroverted leader, but their lack of cheerfulness does not correlate to their leadership skills. Introverted leaders are generally more in tune with their senses and thus can read the emotional cues of people with ease.

The frontal area of the brains of introverts is highly active. This area contains the frontal lobes and the thalamus, areas responsible for various problem solving and thinking activities; therefore, introverted leaders are actually better equipped for making the appropriate decisions even in a time of crisis.

- **Myth #3: Introverts are bad communicators**

Many people often get confused by the way introverts process their ideas differently from extroverts. Many times, this internal processing of ideas can be confusing to extroverts. They may even misjudge introverts and think that they are not interested in the situation. Introverts are methodical thinkers who like to think properly. They tend to go over different scenarios in their minds before coming to a decision. This allows them to be sure of their plans. Once they are sure of their plans, they communicate them to people with full confidence. This is a great way of communicating with people. It is also highly suitable for leadership positions. This allows introverts to present their ideas in a more concrete, well-thought-out, and lucid manner.

- **Myth #4: Introverts don't like collaborating**

It is true that introverts prefer to work alone and that they are highly productive when they are left to their own devices. This does not mean that they cannot work properly on a team, or that they are unable to lead people toward a collaborative goal. Introverted leaders can be especially good in difficult situations.

A study conducted at Harvard University found that extroverted leaders are great for passive teams, but they can be quite problematic for proactive teams. In the latter case, all members of the team are treated equally, and the ideas of all the team members are accepted. Introverts are far more suitable for such teams. As introverts are known for their listening skills, they can help such teams to achieve greater success. Introverts are more receptive to other people's ideas.

Tips for Introverted Leaders

It should now be clear that introverts can become very good leaders. That said, convincing others might take some time. But don't worry, you can move on vigilantly and keep pushing on, determined and confident. Self-confidence is the key to winning big in life.

Many tips can help you become a great introverted leader. In this section, let us have a look at some of these tips one by one.

- **Listen first, talk later**

This is a natural tendency of introverts. Introverts tend to listen a lot more than speak. It is a great skill that can be used in the world of business. If you want to be known and respected as a great leader, you should always pay attention to what other people are saying. You need to listen to what your clients, friends, employees, and followers are trying to tell you. It does not matter who is the best speaker, because the best talkers generally do not have the best ideas.

- **Step up during times of crisis**

Crises and problems are a common part of everyone's life. We all face personal and professional crises from time to time. It does not matter how many crises you face; what matters most is how you face them, and how you respond to things in a time of adversity. A leader needs to be the voice of reason all the time. Even if the ship is sinking, a leader needs to motivate people to save the day. Introverts are blessed with good thinking skills and patience. These two skills are essential in the time of crisis.

- **Get out of your complacent zone**

As explained in a previous chapter, you need to learn how to get out of your complacent zone. If you want to be a leader, you will have to get out of your comfort zone ever so slightly but leave your complacency zone behind. Being a leader involves talking to people and managing them. While you may not like talking to people, if you want to be a successful leader, you will have to do so. Even if you believe that small talk is worthless and hate it, you will still have to do it from time to time. If you find public speaking especially difficult, take a public speaking class. Take the lead on new projects and volunteer to take on new things. Work on yourself every day and move forward gradually. Each week should bring in a new day of personal success for you.

- **Get into your comfort zone**

Introverts love to talk to themselves and think about things. These two things are crucial, along with solitude, for introverts. These sessions allow them to mull things over and relax. A relaxed brain can look at things from various points of view and produce excellent ideas and solutions. So, as a leader, always set some time aside for yourself. It does not need to be an hour; you can even take a 15-minute break and sit alone quietly. Let your thoughts flow and let your body relax completely. If you get any ideas while doing this, don't get up until the session is over. Once the session is over, you can move on to the next tip.

- **Write it down**

Introverts are generally better writers than speakers. This is why you should put your ideas on paper as much as possible before speaking about them. Take some key points and highlight them. This will help you speak clearly and lucidly. Always leave employees with challenging questions, as that will help them perform better.

You may have noticed that certain traits are common in introverts as well as extroverts. Introverts can use their strengths, such as listening and observation skills, to become excellent leaders. If you believe that you have some weaknesses, accept them, and try to work on them. This way, you will become a great leader.

Chapter Nineteen: How Introverts Can Change the World

Responsible citizens of the world who feel that they owe something to society and humanity, often dream of changing the world. They want to make it a better place. Such people want to bring positive changes to the lives of other people. If you are one such person, you want to see the world from a positive point of view. You want people to remember you as a trailblazer and a reformer who changed the lives of people for the greater good. While all of this is quite easy for extroverts, thanks to their outgoing and sociable natures, it can seem quite difficult for introverts, especially if you are one of those people who dislikes even the thought of going out. But this does not mean that you cannot make a difference in the lives of people. It is still possible.

If you are a highly introverted and socially awkward person who wants to change the world but does not know how to start, don't worry; you are not alone. There are many people like you, and there is hope. In this chapter, you will find many tips and suggestions that you can use to learn how to change the world, one step at a time.

Do Most of the Work by Yourself

Introverts do not mind people, but they would rather do things on their own. This is because introverts prefer solitude, and they like to do things at their own pace and while enjoying their own space. If you really want to change the world, understand your pros and tackle your cons.

Changing the world does not mean that you need to get out of the house and organize protests, sit-ins, and marches. You can change the world right from your home. Try to find methods that can help you support the world-changing movements going on outside of your comfort zone. For instance, if people need clothes, you can help them by creating clothing items in your home.

Leave Your Creations as Legacy

Introverts are generally blessed artists. If you are talented and have artistic skills, you can use them to change the world. There are many ways through which you can use art to change the world. Massive conceptual street art installations, photojournalism, or writing thought-pieces are all great avenues by which to leave your mark. If you want to be more local, then arrange art pieces that will connect with the local audience. This way, you will be able to make a difference that you will be able to observe immediately.

If You Do Interact with People, Interact via the Written Word

Introverts are not always great with verbal communication, but they are generally good with written communication. Many writers and famous authors were introverts. If you feel overwhelmed at the prospect of talking to people to change the world, don't worry. Instead of forcing yourself to do something that you find unpleasant, choose methods that will help you achieve the same goals without discomforting you. Instead of delivering speeches in marches, write columns and articles. Your writing can motivate others to move ahead and take things into their own hands. Thus, you will be able to lead a revolution without having to get out of your comfort zone.

Scout Your Surroundings

If you decide to use your art for public demonstration, it's best to scout the area thoroughly before choosing a place to put up your art. This way, you will know how many people will be able to check out your art. Introverts do not like crowds, but if you want to change the world, you need to attract a significant number of people towards your piece.

It's OK to Fail or Avoid Certain Ideas

Introverts like to think a lot, which is why they arrive at exceptional ideas. Many times, it is difficult to make these ideas real. You may dream of making documentaries and art pieces that will change the world (and win good awards), but it does not happen all the time.

Just being an introvert does not mean that you will get ideas that are only suitable for your personality. Many times, introverts get ideas that are far better suited to extroverts. In such cases, introverts rarely act upon these ideas, and the ideas die out. This is because the hustle and bustle involved in bringing these ideas to fruition are taxing, if not impossible to bear, for introverts.

This doesn't mean that you should not think of ambitious ideas. You may feel scared of them now, but times may change, and you may pursue them successfully in the future. If you believe that your idea is too big and scary, try breaking it into chunks and doing it step by step. Or, you can put the big idea aside and start with smaller and simpler ideas instead. Taking small steps and succeeding is far better than taking big steps and failing.

Embrace the Awkward

If you are socially awkward along with being an introvert, don't worry, and instead of hiding your awkwardness, embrace it. Use your awkwardness in a way that will help you send a message to people. Being awkward and feeling awkward is not a negative thing. Rather, it is a sign of growth and development. If you feel awkward doing something, it means that you are doing something that you are not comfortable with. If you feel self-conscious while helping someone, don't worry. Carry on, and soon you will stop feeling strange.

Don't Use Your Introversion as an Excuse

It does not matter whether you are an introvert or an extrovert; anyone can change the world if he or she has the dedication and passion. Instead of blaming your introversion for your inaction, sit down and contemplate why you are not taking any action to change the world. Often, you will find reasons that are not at all related to your introversion. Instead of hiding your introverted characteristics, use them and turn them into assets.

Being an introvert can make a huge difference if you know how to use it. To change the world, you need to act, and to act, you need to get out of your complacent zone. Treat this as a personal growth exercise. If you try to change things for good, you will soon notice them changing. That said, you must try first. If you accept defeat even before trying, then you will never succeed!

So, ultimately, if you want to change the world, change yourself. Make the effort, being bold and confident. Take baby steps if you are not comfortable making huge changes in your own life. With time, you will surely be able to make a difference in the world.

Conclusion

I am sure by now it is clear to you how difficult and confusing an introvert's life can be. It is full of contradictions and complex situations. It is no wonder that introverts tend to stay away from crowds and social gatherings, as those groups are extremely *extrovert* friendly!

One of the most important things that every introvert needs to remember is that introversion is perfectly normal. Many introverts try to change themselves and put a lot of pressure on their brains to become an extrovert. Instead of trying to change, it is better to accept who you are and use your characteristics as assets. If you accept your qualities, you can use them for your benefit.

This book contained many tips and tricks that may help you lead a comfortable introverted life. These tips are tried and tested, and they work. It is recommended that you practice them frequently so that they become habits, allowing you to use them in a far more natural way.

Remember, always be confident and bold, and have patience. Be yourself, and the world will love you.

References

https://www.learning-mind.com/4-introvert-types-which-one-are-you/

https://thriveglobal.com/stories/25-signs-that-tell-you-are-an-introvert%EF%BB%BF/

https://www.mindfulnessmuse.com/individual-differences/myers-briggs-8-introverted-personality-types

https://introvertdear.com/what-it-feels-like-to-be-an-introvert/

https://introvertspring.com/15-introvert-myths-busted/

https://www.elegantthemes.com/blog/business/famous-introverts-and-what-you-can-learn-from-them

http://www.magicaldaydream.com/2015/09/7-tips-on-how-to-change-the-world-if-youre-an-introverted-unicorn.html

https://thehustle.co/why-introverts-make-great-leaders/

https://www.lifehack.org/articles/communication/5-simple-and-effective-leadership-tips-for-introverts.html

https://www.scienceofpeople.com/introvert/

https://www.trade-schools.net/articles/best-jobs-for-introverts.asp

https://psych2go.net/10-things-introverts-need-relationship/

https://psych2go.net/6-relationship-tips-for-introverts/

https://www.huffpost.com/entry/how-to-network-introvert_l_5d13d8c2e4b0d0a2c0ab3e92

https://www.forbes.com/sites/jonlevy/2018/04/20/8-networking-tips-for-introverts-from-a-superconnector/#60845ca226ef

https://introvertdear.com/news/introverts-guide-making-friends-get/

https://www.valgeisler.com/11-perfectly-introverted-ways-to-make-friends-as-an-adult/

https://introvertspring.com/how-to-make-friends-if-youre-an-introvert/

https://www.quietrev.com/the-4-differences-between-introversion-and-social-anxiety/

https://themighty.com/2019/03/introvert-with-social-anxiety-what-to-know/

https://www.elitedaily.com/p/how-introverts-can-make-small-talk-less-painful-more-meaningful-according-to-experts-8917603

https://www.lifehack.org/articles/lifestyle/7-epic-strategies-for-introverts-by-introverts-to-ignite-your-social-skills.html

http://elitemanmagazine.com/10-tips-to-becoming-more-social-as-an-introvert/

https://www.wikihow.com/Be-Socially-Confident

https://introvertdear.com/news/anxious-introverts-fears/

https://psych2go.net/5-steps-to-overcome-your-fears-as-an-introvert/

https://introvertdear.com/news/introverts-happy-need/

https://www.verywellmind.com/how-to-be-a-happy-introvert-1717557

https://introvertdear.com/news/introverts-alone-time-science-marti-olsen-laney/

https://psychcentral.com/lib/introverts-and-the-quest-for-quiet/

https://blog.dropbox.com/topics/work-culture/introverts-quiet-time-creativity

https://introvertspring.com/the-truth-about-introvert-anxiety-and-depression/

https://www.familyaddictionspecialist.com/blog/how-mental-health-issues-may-differ-among-introverts-and-extroverts

https://introvertdear.com/news/5-reasons-introverts-mental-health-plan/

https://jenniferrabin.com/introverts-can-change-world/

Check out another book by Daron Callaway

SOCIAL
ANXIETY

DISCOVER HOW TO QUIET YOUR NEGATIVE THOUGHTS, OVERCOME WORRY, BUILD YOUR SOCIAL SKILLS, AND CURE SHYNESS SO YOU CAN HAVE SMALL TALK WITH EASE EVEN AS AN INTROVERT

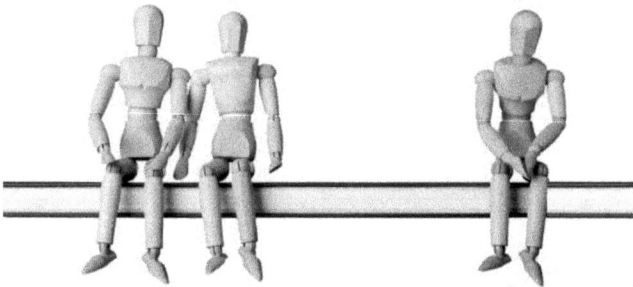

DARON CALLAWAY

www.ingramcontent.com/pod-product-compliance
Lightning Source LLC
Chambersburg PA
CBHW070759300326
41914CB00053B/743